A Daughter's INHERITANCE

From Survival to Safety:
A Mother's Choice to Break the Cycle

TAMMY BLAKE

LANDON
HAIL
PRESS

Paperback ISBN: 978-1-959955-85-6
Hardback ISBN: 978-1-959955-86-3

Published by Landon Hail Press
Cover design by Rich Johnson, Spectacle Photo
Photos by Angelli Nguyen

For the child I used to be. You bloomed.
For the ones rebuilding themselves from silence ~ I see you.
And for my daughter, you are the beautiful bridge.

CONTENTS

A MESSAGE FOR THE READER

To the woman holding this book ~

I already know you're brave, because you're here.

Maybe you're carrying grief no one sees.

Maybe you're healing things your family still refuses to name.

Maybe you're the one who always keeps it together, even while something inside you is quietly unraveling.

This book is not a step-by-step guide or a polished testimony.

It's the lived truth of what happened when I stopped surviving and let God lead me into healing.

There are pieces of my story in these pages—

the ache of being unseen,

the weight of what was never named,

the slow, sacred process of coming back to myself.

If something in here meets you…

if a sentence lingers, or a memory stirs, or a truth quietly lands—

I hope you let it.

I hope you feel less alone.

I hope you feel seen in places that have gone unseen for too long.

And I just want to say—thank you for being here.

Thank you for holding this story.

For allowing these words—and me—to take up space with you.

This is my offering.

My surrender.

My lived experience.

My story.

And if something in your soul whispered, this is for me—
it is.

AUTHOR'S NOTE

This book began as a quiet whisper in my spirit—a nudge from God that said, "Write what you've healed."

I didn't know then that every sentence would become a prayer, every page a piece of my becoming. At the heart of it all is my daughter—the reason I said yes to healing, the reason I keep choosing truth over comfort and faith over fear. Healing is the inheritance I'm leaving her. Faith is the foundation it's built on. She deserves a mother who is whole, not half-hidden; a mother who leads with peace, not performance. Every boundary I've set, every tear I've cried, and every prayer I've whispered has been so she can grow up knowing love that doesn't wound, faith that doesn't shame, and safety that doesn't disappear when life gets hard.

But this story isn't only for her. It's for the little girl inside me who spent years trying to earn love she already had. She, too, deserves healing. She deserves to be seen, held, and freed from the patterns that once kept her small. Writing these pages has been my way of mothering her—of saying, "You made it home."

And it's for every woman who has ever felt unseen, unheard, or unloved. For the chosen family God has woven into my life—the sisters, mentors, and friends who became

His proof that I was never alone. Through them, I've witnessed what real love looks like: steady, safe, and sacred.

This book is a testimony to the God who gave me everything I didn't have—not in the way I expected, but in the way I needed. It's a love letter to the generations after me, a promise that the story can change. That healing can become heritage. That peace can be passed down.

So, to my daughter, to the girl I once was, and to every woman still finding her way home—this is for you. May you remember that your story, too, is holy. And may you always trust the One who writes redemption into every line.

"People will speak about your life
without ever sitting with your story.
God gave me the courage to tell it anyway."

INTRODUCTION

The Day My Voice Was Called to the Stand

I was old enough to know fear but young enough that my feet still dangled from the courtroom bench. I remember the cold. The fluorescent lights. The stillness that made even my breath feel too loud.

But mostly, I remember her.

My attorney.

Tall. Composed. Wrapped in a blue suit that felt like the safest thing in the room.

Her name was Dixie—a name that etched itself into my memory like it had always belonged there, like it was waiting for me before I even had words for what I was living through.

I remember riding up in the elevator with her. Just her and me.

I was just a little girl trying to make sense of something far too big for me. I was there, but so much of it felt out of my hands.

I don't know who took me to the courthouse.

I don't remember if anyone thanked this woman for guiding a scared little girl into a place designed for adults.

Trauma blurs everything except what it wants you to remember. And I remembered her.

Her hair—bright, almost platinum blonde—resting at her shoulders.

I thought she was so beautiful. So sophisticated.

She felt like a calm anchor while the room swallowed the rest of me completely.

I remember the echo of heels.

Papers shuffling.

The hum of something too official for a child who still sucked her thumb and slept with stuffed animals tucked under her chin.

And I remember the way everyone looked at me—

not with softness,

not with protection,

but with scrutiny.

Judgment.

As if the harm done to me was something I had caused.

As if a child could be guilty for her own abuse.

Even now, I don't fully understand why I had to be there.

Why I had to sit in that room and carry something that was never mine to hold.

I focused on Dixie. Because she was the only thing in the room that didn't make me feel like I had done something wrong.

She stood beside me—steady, grounded—while I faced something I didn't yet understand.

And I didn't know it then, but that moment would stay with me for a very, very long time. Because it wouldn't be the last time I had to find my voice in a room that wasn't built to hold it.

PART ONE

THE MAKING OF A QUIET GIRL

CHAPTER 1

Silent Lessons: The Girl Who Read the Room

I learned to read people before I learned to read books. Long before math or spelling, I learned how to decode a room like a language. Tone became my alphabet. Footsteps were punctuation. Silence was a full sentence. I didn't know it at the time—I thought every child could feel when something wasn't right before it was said out loud, but now I understand this was the beginning of something much deeper. This was the birth of my two selves—the girl the world saw, and the girl who knew too much.

At school, I was easygoing—the sweet one, the well-behaved one, the smiley one. I blended in, laughed at the right moments, and mirrored whatever the room needed from me. Teachers enjoyed me because I was polite and "easy." I didn't cause problems or take up space. I was helpful, responsible, trustworthy—the kind of girl adults praised without ever really knowing. No one knew I was performing safety. No one knew it wasn't personality at all, just survival.

There was a season, though—around fourth and fifth grade—when something in me pushed back. I remember getting in trouble for talking too much, for being disruptive. The "class clown," they called me, and I remember liking how it felt. When I made people laugh, something in me lit up. For a moment, I wasn't invisible. I wasn't trying to read the room—I was changing it. I think I just wanted to be seen, to feel important, to feel like I mattered.

I went to the same private school from preschool through twelfth grade. At the time, I didn't fully understand why I loved it so much—I just knew I did. Now I know it was because it was the one thing in my life that stayed the same. The same hallways, the same classrooms, the same small group of kids growing up together year after year. These weren't people I vaguely remembered—they were people I knew deeply. We grew up together, and there was something really special about that.

Second grade stands out in my memory. My teacher, Mrs. O, was beautiful to me—not just in how she looked, but in the way she made me feel. I always wanted to be near her. I remember trying to get to the front of the line so I could walk right behind her, or beside her if I could. I wanted to be close enough to be noticed. And she did notice me, or I wouldn't have felt the way I did—safe, happy, seen. I remember telling her she was my favorite teacher. I remember how she smelled, how she spoke to me, how it felt to be in her presence. Looking back, I think she filled something in me I didn't yet have words for.

School was one world. Home was another.

At home, I wasn't the smiley one. I was alert—hyper-aware, anxious, always braced for impact. My mother's tone dictated everything—the slam of a cabinet, the shift in her breathing, the smell of alcohol the moment she opened her mouth. Every sound told me what kind of night it was going to be. That was when hypervigilance became a second skin. I learned to scan everything—every doorway, every sound, every silence. I learned that danger often comes quietly before it comes loud, so I became quiet too, not because that was who I was, but because it felt safer to be.

At home, it was mostly just me and my mom. My dad was a truck driver and gone more often than he was there, and even when he was home, it felt like he lived somewhere else entirely.

Later, when my stepdad moved in, it didn't make things clearer—it made them more confusing. No one explained anything. Not who he was, not what was happening, not why my mom drank the way she did. We didn't talk about anything. We just lived inside it. I learned to stay in line, stay quiet, and stay out of the way.

There is one memory from that time that still lives in my chest like a bruise.

I was maybe eleven or twelve. My mother was drunk again—yelling, raging, unleashing whatever storm the alcohol had stirred inside her. Something in me snapped that night. Maybe it was fear. Maybe it was exhaustion. Maybe it was the smallest, trembling belief that someone outside those four walls could help me.

I remember grabbing the phone—the old landline—running downstairs, and hiding in the hallway by the ping-pong room. I didn't know what number to call. I didn't know what to say. I only knew I needed help.

She screamed my name from upstairs. "Tammmmyyyyy!"

I froze.

Every cell in my body went cold. I was certain she was coming down those stairs to hurt me. I didn't call the agency like I thought I would. I didn't know how. Instead, I did the only thing my body trusted.

I called my Grandma Betty.

She came. Of course, she came. She always did.

I can still hear her car pulling into the driveway. I remember getting into the car—it was cold, but the moment I sat on those yellow leather seats, something in me softened. I knew I was safe. I knew I wasn't going to get yelled at. I knew that, for just a little while, everything was going to be okay.

Grandma Betty—God's Whisper in a Yellow Cadillac:

If my mother was chaos, my Grandma Betty was calm.

She was my dad's mom—my angel on earth—the one who made me feel so deeply loved. She saved me more times than I can count. Being with her felt like stepping out of a storm and into a soft, quiet room. My shoulders dropped. My breathing slowed. My body knew it was safe.

At home, things often felt tense and unpredictable. I didn't always feel settled or at ease. With Grandma, I was nurtured. I was welcomed. I was enough just as I was. She was gentle and steady—the kind of calm that made me believe love actually existed.

One of my most beautiful, clearest memories with her is going to Kmart. We would always stop in the cafeteria for a Coke and sit together at those little tables that smelled faintly of fried food and coffee. I can still smell it.

But more than anything, I remember her reaching for my hand.

Even walking into the store, down the aisles, into the cafeteria—she always held my hand. It was my favorite thing. I didn't know then how much it meant. Her hands were always a little cold, but they were so beautiful to me. She wore rings, and I can still hear the soft clink of them against the steering wheel when she drove.

She paid attention to me. She asked me questions. She listened to my answers. She didn't rush me or dismiss me. She saw me.

I remember ordering food and then looking up at her, quietly asking without words, *Is this okay?* And if she said yes, she gave me something I didn't even realize I was missing—permission. Permission to take up space. Permission to choose. Permission to exist without fear.

Those ordinary moments are imprinted in my nervous system as deeply as any trauma.

God gave me those moments through her—a whisper of what love could feel like... and did feel like. I didn't have it at home, but I tasted it there, in the cafeteria at Kmart. And somehow, that made it sacred.

She drove a yellow Cadillac, and I loved that car like it was a character in my life story. Grandma always drove. Grandpa sat in the back. I rode shotgun, feeling chosen. We took trips to Lubbock, Texas, and places I don't even fully remember now, but it never mattered where we were going. What I remember is laughing about nothing—playing games in the car, giggling when we read the map wrong. I loved the feeling of being with them. I could feel they were proud of me and that I was deeply loved.

I was their only granddaughter—or at least that's how it felt. I loved her jewelry, her hair appointments, the way she carried herself with quiet grace. I can still see her rings, her earrings, the dignity she moved through the world with.

Looking back now, I realize how holy she really was in my story.

Grandma Betty wasn't just my safe place—she was God's whisper to me long before I had language for Him. Living proof that gentleness was real. That love didn't have to hurt. That steadiness was possible. That attention and affection were not wrong.

I sent you Grandma Betty, so you would know
what love feels like… what safety feels like…
So it would imprint on your heart forever.

CHAPTER 2

Claiborne Street

When I think about my childhood, I think about that cul-de-sac. That's where my nervous system learned what home was—and what it wasn't.

Our house sat there, dark and unsettled, though I didn't have those words then. I just knew I wanted it to feel safe. I needed it to feel safe. But it didn't.

From the time I was about six through my mid-teens, that house held a tension I couldn't name—only feel. So, I adapted.

What I remember most about that neighborhood isn't our home. It's everyone else's.

I created a sense of home everywhere but my own.

As a child, I instinctively placed myself inside other people's lives. I found safety wherever it was offered—sometimes, intentionally; sometimes without even realizing it. I didn't know what I was doing. I just knew where my body could soften, where I could breathe, and where I felt wanted… or useful.

There were certain houses that felt different. One of them stood out in a quiet, steady way. The parents were older, and their home felt calm in a way I wasn't used to. I loved caring for their daughter. I felt trusted there—seen in quiet ways that didn't require anything from me.

Next door lived Laura and Dallas and their daughter, Kayli. I adored that family. Laura was warm and beautiful, and she liked me—that mattered more than I understood at the time. I babysat often, went shopping with them, and even got to go to Wichita Wings games, because Dallas played on the team. I remember thinking it was the coolest thing—being part of that energy, the excitement of knowing someone on the field. I felt included with them, which was special—like I was part of something bigger, just because he was a player.

That's why what happened later confused me so deeply. I was about fifteen or sixteen when it happened. He was a married man, and I was a young girl, his babysitter.

At the time, I didn't have language for what it was. I just remember feeling confused. Part of me felt flattered, almost in disbelief that this was happening, and another part of me didn't fully understand why it didn't feel right.

Looking back now, I can see it clearly. He was a grown man who took advantage of a teenage girl. But at the time, I didn't see it that way—I just felt caught in something I didn't know how to make sense of.

The safety I'd thought I had there was gone.

Around the block were other homes—some I barely entered. Quiet houses. Closed doors. The Goldens' house felt darker somehow. Both of the parents were teachers, and they had a lot of kids—or at least it felt like they did. I remember music in their basement—The Cure, Depeche Mode, Siouxsie and the Banshees. Posters. Dim lighting. It felt older, heavier.

Then there were the Whitmans. The big white house on the curve. My childhood friend Kara lived there. I remember sleepovers that ended early—moments when something in my body told me to leave. I didn't understand it then. I just listened.

The Taylors lived nearby, too. My friend Lila's mom had a beautiful accent—I think it was Scottish. What stood out most to me was how much she loved her own mother—how she wanted to stay close to her. That confused me. I couldn't understand wanting to be near your mom like that. That kind of connection felt foreign.

At the end of the street was another house. I became friends with a girl there named Hannah. At first, it felt like any other friendship, but over time, something about it felt off. Even as a kid, I could sense it. There was always a lot of talk around that house—things I didn't fully understand, but I could feel the tension of it. Looking back, I can see how manipulative that dynamic was, but at the time, I just knew it didn't feel steady.

It was also in one of those houses that I began to notice the difference between innocence and something else—though I didn't have language for that yet, either.

Between our house and my best friend Avery's stood another home. My first kiss happened there, inside a small doghouse. We were young. It was brief and innocent. I remember it because it felt simple. Safe.

There were eleven houses on that cul-de-sac, including ours. Out of the other ten, I slept in at least seven. Sometimes, because I was babysitting. Sometimes, because I was staying over with friends.

But most of the time, it was because I felt safer there than I did at home.

I didn't know it then, but I was building safety wherever I could find it. I was learning how to create a sense of home… even when I didn't have one.

And later—years later—I would look back and realize:

He was there when I learned to read rooms. He was there when I learned to survive. He was there when I started living two lives. He was there when I thought I was alone.

I gave you safe places to land…, so your heart would recognize what was real, even in the middle of what wasn't.

CHAPTER 3

When Being Good Stopped Working

There wasn't a single moment when everything changed. It happened slowly, quietly. The same things that once helped me feel safe started to wear me down, but I didn't recognize it at the time. I just kept going.

By the time I was a teenager, being "good" wasn't just something I did. It was who I was. It had worked its way into everything—how I spoke, how I acted, what I noticed, and what I carried. I knew how to read people in the sense that I could feel what was needed before it was said. I knew how to anticipate, how to step in, how to make things easier. I also knew how to disappear when things felt tense and come back when things needed fixing.

What I didn't realize was how exhausted I was. Not the kind of tired that sleep fixes, but the kind that sits in your chest. The kind that comes from never fully resting because resting doesn't feel safe. The kind that comes from always being on watch.

I didn't rebel. I didn't act out. I didn't collapse. I just kept going.

That was the problem.

The adults around me called it strength. They said I was mature for my age. Responsible. Capable. They trusted me. They leaned on me. They praised me for handling things most kids shouldn't have to handle.

No one questioned why I was able to.

No one asked what it cost.

At home, the chaos continued—unpredictable, loud, fueled by alcohol and volatility. I learned to sense danger before it spoke. I learned to soften my presence, to manage moods, to intervene when I could and endure when I couldn't. I learned that being invisible was sometimes safer than being seen.

But something began to crack inside me during those years.

Not loudly. Not dramatically.

It cracked in the way I stopped knowing what I wanted. In the way joy felt unfamiliar. In the way I could take care of everyone else but didn't know how to take care of myself. In the way I felt responsible for outcomes that were never mine to control.

I carried guilt that didn't belong to me. Shame that wasn't earned. A sense of obligation that felt holy but wasn't.

I didn't know yet that I was confusing survival with virtue. I didn't know yet that I was allowed to be more than useful.

And still—even here—God remained.

Not as rescue. Not as answers. But as restraint. As the quiet line that kept me from disappearing completely. As the unseen hand that kept placing people, moments, small mercies in my path—enough to survive, not yet enough to heal.

Healing would come later.

First, I had to reach the end of what being good could do for me.

Caretaking didn't stop when I left childhood. It followed me into adolescence the way muscle memory does—quietly, automatically, without my consent. By then, it wasn't something I did. It was who I was.

I learned early on how to make myself useful in other people's lives. How to anticipate needs. How to notice what was missing before anyone else named it. That instinct carried me into the homes I babysat in, into friendships, and into relationships that felt safer than those in my own house ever had.

I didn't just babysit. I stepped into whatever was needed.

I remember opening fridges and noticing what was missing without anyone saying it. Straightening things as I went. Paying attention to the mood in the room—whether it felt calm or tense, whether someone was overwhelmed or just tired.

I didn't think about it at the time. I just moved with it.

It felt normal to me—to step in, to help, to make things easier wherever I could.

Looking back, I can see what that really was. It wasn't maturity the way people thought it was. It was survival.

On Claiborne Street, I moved between houses more than I stayed in my own. I knew where I was welcome and where I was needed. And over time, those places started to feel more like home than mine did.

That pattern followed me into my first real relationship—one that grew out of the same neighborhood, the same season, the same longing to be chosen and kept. We were young when it started, barely old enough to know what we were promising each other, and it lasted nearly a decade. Ten years of learning how to stay, how to accommodate, and how to bend without breaking—or at least without leaving. Even when our lives tangled and untangled, even when we lived together and then didn't, caretaking remained my posture. I didn't yet know how to ask whether a relationship was good for me. I only knew how to make it work.

Looking back, I can see how deeply this role had fused with my sense of worth. Being needed felt like safety. Being useful felt like belonging. Love, to me, meant paying attention, staying alert, and making things easier for others—even when it made me disappear.

There were moments when my body tried to speak before I had language for it. Moments when something inside me froze or recoiled or went quiet, even when my mouth didn't say no. I didn't understand those signals then. I didn't know they were warnings. I only knew how to override them—the same way I had learned to override fear, discomfort, and confusion at home.

I didn't yet have the words for what had been taken from me or for how that unspoken wound shaped the way I attached, stayed, and cared. I only knew that, somewhere along the way, being good had cost me my spontaneity, my innocence, and my ability to trust my own instincts. And still—I kept caring. I kept managing. I kept surviving.

This was the version of love I knew how to offer.

And then, somewhere along the way, I found a place where being needed didn't feel confusing.

It felt right.

It felt like love.

The first was my grandpa. He was gruff in the way men of his generation often were—worked hard, didn't say much, carried himself like a man who had spent years getting things done. I always imagined him that way in his working life—no nonsense, steady, respected.

But the grandpa I knew was softer than that.

He had this old green recliner—the kind that had been sat in for years, worn in all the right places. That's where he would be most evenings, watching TV, drifting in and out of sleep. I would sit behind his chair, gently rubbing his bald head until he stirred. Sometimes I'd try to wake him on purpose just to see his reaction.

He never got annoyed. He would just open his eyes, look at me, and smile—like it was our own little game.

I remember tying red balloons to his head with the neighbor girl, Barbie, because they would just sit there perfectly on his bald head. We thought it was hilarious. And he let us. Every time.

He had an old neck injury from when he was younger. His neck stayed tilted to the side—he couldn't hold it upright. It was just... who he was to me. I never questioned it. I never saw it as anything but him. And I loved him exactly the way he was.

The safest place I knew as a child was their backyard. Even now, I can still smell the honeysuckle.

It was the kind of place that felt bright and soft at the same time—like nothing bad could reach you there. There was a small shed, a wide yard, and this quiet sense of peace that I didn't have anywhere else.

When I was older, sitting in therapy years later, I was asked to picture a safe place—somewhere I could go when things got too overwhelming, when the trauma got too loud.

I didn't have to think long. I went right back there. To that backyard.

To the smell of honeysuckle. To the feeling of being safe.

One of my favorite memories is riding on his lawnmower. It was this small, butter-yellow mower that felt like the coolest thing in the world to me. I would sit right in front of him while he drove, even though I couldn't reach anything. He would let me hold on, like I was part of it, like I was helping.

We'd ride through the yard, through the little gate, making slow circles. I remember the sound of it, the rhythm, the way it felt to be right there with him.

Clementine, their huge Saint Bernard, would be nearby—this giant, gentle dog I treated like my own personal horse. I rode him, hugged him, and followed him around like he was part of the magic of that place.

And every New Year's Eve, we had our tradition.

Without fail, my grandma would come over to me just before midnight and whisper, "You wanna go get some saucepans?"

And my whole face would light up.

We'd grab pots and pans, a wooden spoon, and wait for the clock to hit midnight. And then—right on cue—we would start marching in circles through the house, banging and laughing and shouting, "Happy New Year! Happy New Year!"

We'd loop through the den and the kitchen over and over, making as much noise as we could. And it startled my grandpa every single time.

He'd wake up, confused, half-smiling, asking, "What are you girls doing?"

And we would just laugh and laugh.

Those memories stayed with me. They still do.

And thank God they did.

Because, years later, when I sat in that hospital room with him—the cold air, the sterile smell, the quiet hum of machines—I needed something to hold onto.

And those were the moments I went back to.

By then, when his health began to decline, I was in my late twenties. I don't remember every medical detail—what exactly they called it or how it all unfolded—but I remember the feeling of it. The urgency. The weight. The knowing that something serious was happening.

My grandma was sick, too. COPD had taken so much from her, and she couldn't be at the hospital the way she wanted to. So, I stepped in without hesitation. I became the one who showed up, who listened, and who made sure nothing was missed.

I remember walking into that hospital room for the first time—the cold air, the steady hum of machines, the quiet that didn't feel peaceful. I watched the nurses closely. I listened to every word the doctors said, trying to understand what was happening.

At some point, I was given power of attorney over his medical decisions. I remember how clearly that moment landed. I didn't feel overwhelmed by it—I felt ready.

Honored. Like I had been handed something important, something that mattered.

Looking back now, I can see how much of my identity wrapped itself around that role. But at the time, it just felt natural. Of course I would do this. Of course I would take care of him.

I even printed out the paperwork and brought it with me to the hospital, because it felt important for me to do that—like proof that I was supposed to take care of him. More than once, I stayed overnight in that room, down the hall from my grandpa—barely sleeping, just knowing I needed to be there in case anything happened. I remember feeling so responsible and so brave, and also scared at the same time.

When I stayed overnight, I slept lightly, listening for changes, making sure he was okay. I asked questions. I spoke up. I paid attention in ways that felt instinctive, not learned.

And in a life where so much felt uncertain, this was something I could hold onto. Something I could do well. Something that made me feel needed in a way that felt steady instead of chaotic.

I remember the small things more than anything else. The way the room felt late at night. The stillness of everything around us. The weight of being the one responsible.

I remember my Aunt Helen bringing me the cutest panda candle—something small and soft in a place that felt anything but. I remember how much that meant to me. How seen I felt in that moment.

It's funny how you remember the people who loved you gently. The ones who showed up in small, steady ways. She was one of those people for me.

And with my grandpa, caretaking didn't feel like survival. It felt like devotion.

If taking care of my grandpa felt like purpose, taking care of my grandma felt softer. More intimate. And heavier in a way I didn't fully understand at the time.

She wasn't in a hospital. She was at home, exactly where she wanted to be, and I was there with her, hour after hour and day after day, until the very end. I didn't live there, but it felt like I did. I showed up every day, stayed overnight more times than I can count, and somewhere along the way, that house became the center of everything.

The house on Brookside. I can still picture it and feel it so vividly, because that's where I felt most safe. I played there as a little girl, up in the attic, with a black cash register of my grandma's, plus bins full of toys. I absolutely loved being up there—it felt like its own little world.

My grandma was everything to me. My grandpa was loving and steady, but my grandma… she could do no wrong in my eyes. She was gentle in a way that felt safe—the kind of safe that didn't need to be explained.

Before she got really sick, we did everything together. I took her to her doctor's appointments, her hair appointments. We shopped—Kmart, always Kmart, and then later TJ Maxx. That's where I fell in love with TJ Maxx, just walking the aisles with her, being with her. Those were some of my favorite moments.

She only lived about eight months after my grandpa passed, and in those eight months, I did everything I knew how to do to take care of her.

She missed him so much. You could feel it in the house—in the quiet, in the way she moved. And on top of that, her body was slowly giving out from COPD. She had smoked those long, skinny, brown cigarettes for years, and it had taken its toll in the worst way.

But even in that, she was still her—still kind, still beautiful, still put together in her own way. Leopard prints, gorgeous colors, her jewelry. I always admired that about her, and I still do. She carried herself with a quiet dignity that I didn't understand then, but I see so clearly now.

She was the one who taught me how to be in the world. She taught me to say please and thank you, to open doors for people, to let others go first, to be kind even when it wasn't returned. I don't remember her sitting me down and explaining it—she just lived it, and I absorbed it.

And I loved her for that.

Taking care of her in those final months was the hardest thing I've ever done. I helped her walk to the bathroom and back to the couch. I gave her morphine when she needed it. I did whatever I could to ease her pain, to make her comfortable, to give her even a little bit of peace.

That couch became her bed—the brown paisley one she loved and had for years. And I made a little place for myself right next to her on the floor. That's where I stayed.

I didn't think about it or question it—I just did it, because that's what love looked like to me. There were days I would leave her house completely wrecked, so sad I didn't know what to do with it.

And instead of processing it, instead of feeling it, I would numb it. I would drink. I would try to quiet everything inside of me that felt too big, too heavy. Then, I would wake up the next day and go right back—back to her, back to that house, back to taking care of her like nothing inside of me was breaking.

I didn't have the tools to do it any other way.

The day she passed is something I will never forget. We had been together all day. At some point, we laid down to take a nap on the couch. Just the two of us.

And when I woke up, she didn't.

I remember saying, "Grandma… Grandma…," and she wasn't there anymore. It was absolutely the most gut-wrenching feeling—to know in that moment she was gone. The one human who had poured so much love into me—the safest person I had known my entire life—was just gone.

I remember asking her neighbor, Doreen, to come over. I didn't know what else to do, and I couldn't be alone in that moment. So, she came over and helped me.

At some point, I asked her if she would take a picture of me with my grandma. I didn't think about it. I didn't question it. I just knew I wanted it.

Looking back, I've wondered if that was strange. I think a part of me felt even then, maybe it wasn't something people would understand. But I also know now I didn't do it for anyone else. I did it because I loved her.

I have that picture still. It's right here next to me as I write this. Me, lying beside her on that couch, holding her in my arms.

And as hard as that moment was, it also feels sacred to me. I was there. She wasn't alone. And somehow, that matters more than anything else.

Her funeral was another moment etched in me. My body was shaking, but I knew I had to say something. I had to honor her with sharing what a beautiful soul she was.

She had loved me so gently for so long, I don't think I fully understood how much of my safety lived inside her.

And I remember feeling like I had to dim that. Like I couldn't fully express what she meant to me. My mother was watching, and our relationship had always been complicated. There had been unkind words over the years about my grandma and me—words that tried to make something beautiful feel wrong.

But to me, she was my safe place. And those words never changed that—they just made it hurt more.

I remember my Uncle Rodney crying, my teddy bear in human form thanking me for taking care of her. Telling me how much he loved me, and how much it meant.

And then came the contrast between that and the man I thought was my father. The absence. The lack of care. The inability to show up in any meaningful way.

So, I did. I showed up. I took care of her, because that's what I knew how to do. And even now, when I think about that season, there isn't an ounce of regret.

It was exhausting. It was overwhelming. It broke me in ways I didn't understand at the time. But I wouldn't have done it any differently.

She deserved to be loved like that, and I loved her with everything I had.

Somewhere in the middle of all that grief and heartache, I started to fall apart. At the time, I didn't have language for any of it. I just knew I was hurting, and I didn't know what to do with that kind of pain. So, I started using alcohol as a crutch, and before long, I became dependent on it.

Everything in my life began to unravel. I couldn't keep a job. I was searching for connection in all the wrong places, looking for something—someone—to fill a void I didn't yet understand. I felt completely alone.

Those were my duplex years. A lot of that time is still blurry, but I remember enough to know how lost I was.

After my grandma passed, there wasn't anywhere for all of that grief to go. And the relationship with my mom during that time only made things harder. We were constantly at odds, trying to communicate but never quite reaching each other. Everything felt unstable. Unsafe.

I didn't have the words for it then, but looking back now, I can see how deep that wound really was.

Alcohol had a strong hold on me. It was already in my bloodline, and at some point, it took hold of me, too.

I remember one night at the duplex, lying on the couch in excruciating pain. I couldn't breathe. I didn't know what was happening, but I knew something was seriously wrong. I ended up calling for help, and an ambulance came to get me. It was pancreatitis—one of the worst experiences of my life.

I remember lying there, alone, wondering if I was going to die. And if I did, who would even know—or care.

Eventually, it all caught up to me. I didn't want to call it addiction. I fought that word hard. The idea that I might never be able to drink again felt almost impossible to imagine. At the time, it overwhelmed me completely. But deep down, I knew something had to change.

One moment—July 2010—is etched in me.

I had blacked out again, and when I came to, something inside me was different. I was sitting in my living room, exhausted, hurting, and completely broken.

And in that moment, I heard a quiet voice inside me say, *I know you can do this.*

I didn't know it was God at the time. I just knew I believed it.

So, I called, and somehow, I was able to get in the next week.

No one forced me. No one gave me an ultimatum. I chose it.

I called a women's recovery program nearby where I lived, scared, hopeful, and determined to find help. That decision is still one of the most important moments of my life.

Walking into rehab was one of the hardest things I've ever done. I was physically, mentally, and emotionally depleted. But, somewhere underneath all of that, there was a small piece of hope. And that was enough.

I learned a lot during that time, but there's one moment that stuck with me. I remember seeing a girl at a payphone. She looked young and tough—like she didn't need anyone—but something in me said, *Go talk to her.*

So, I did. And somehow, years later, she became one of my chosen people. My beautiful Blakely. We stood in each other's weddings, had babies around the same time, and walked through some deeply real seasons together. She is still one of the safest friendships of my life.

Funny how one of the hardest places I've ever been gave me one of the best friendships of my life. God really does have a way of planting something beautiful in the most unexpected places, like a friendship that is still part of my life today.

The people who find you in your break often
become the ones who stay.

CHAPTER 4

The Slow Unraveling:

Silence as a Second Skin

After rehab, everything was quieter—but not necessarily easier.

I wasn't drinking anymore, but I also wasn't fully rooted in who I was yet. I was learning how to live again. Learning how to feel. Learning how to trust myself in a way I never had before.

It was a tender season. Honest. Fragile in ways I didn't always recognize.

I wasn't looking for anything dramatic. I wasn't chasing chaos anymore. I just wanted something that felt steady. Safe. Different from what I had known.

And when I met him, that's exactly what it seemed like.

By the time I reached my mid-thirties, I thought I had finally arrived somewhere safe. Not because life had become loud or joyful or expansive—but because it had gone quiet. The chaos I grew up with inside had softened into predictability. The volatility had been replaced with routine.

After years of vigilance, my nervous system finally exhaled and mistook that for peace. I didn't yet understand that safety and stillness aren't the same thing. I only knew my body stopped bracing, and for the first time, that felt like rest.

I didn't fall into silence overnight. I was trained into it—shaped by it—until it fit like a second skin.

It wasn't dramatic at first. It didn't look like heartbreak from the outside. It looked like a life. It looked like stability. It looked like a man who didn't yell, didn't rage, didn't drink, didn't demand.

And after the kind of childhood I came from, that felt like the miracle I had been waiting for.

I didn't know then that quiet can be a hiding place. I didn't know that stillness can be mistaken for safety. I just knew my nervous system exhaled around him—and I called that love.

What didn't work—and I can laugh about it now, but barely—is that I immediately found a guy who reminded me of my dad and decided to date him.

Not almost.

I *did* date him.

And, of course, I found myself right back inside a toxic triangle—being chosen second again. Familiar pain. Familiar confusion. Familiar ache. The kind that doesn't feel dramatic, just exhausting. The kind where you think, *I can't do this again,* but somehow you still do.

I'll never forget December 8. My birthday.

It was 2010 or maybe 2011, right after I got out of rehab.

I thought my head was clear. That my choices would be different.

They weren't.

I was wearing this silly little green hat with a frog on it—I don't even know where it came from—and I was crying so hard, my body felt like it might split in two. He broke my heart. Not in a loud way. In a quiet, devastating way that left me hollow and embarrassed and so deeply tired.

I didn't want to kill myself—but I didn't want to be alive either. I remember feeling confused in my head, untethered, like my life was ending and I couldn't explain why. I knew something was very wrong, but I didn't have language for it yet.

I didn't know what to do, so I just left. I knew I needed to get away from him.

I remember driving down the highway, completely wrecked, tears streaming, heart shattered. I called my friend and was sobbing so hard, I could barely get words out. What gutted me wasn't just the heartbreak—it was the shame. I couldn't believe I was here again. Another unhealthy situation. Another rejection. Another version of myself choosing something that made me feel small.

And here's the part that matters most:

I didn't drink.

I didn't drink.

That alone tells me how fragile—and how powerful—that season really was.

I was fresh out of rehab. I had no real coping skills yet. No tools. No language for what my nervous system was doing. Liquor stores on every corner. Old patterns waiting for me like they always had. And still—I didn't drink.

That night, my body was in full fight-or-flight mode, even though I didn't know that term yet. I just knew I couldn't stay where I was, so I left. I checked into a cheap hotel and stood in front of the mirror, staring at myself. I was wrecked. Tear-stained. Raw. And somehow—still—I looked kind of cute. Frog hat and all.

And even in the middle of all that pain, I knew something else, too: This was going to be okay—just not right now.

I cried deep, body-breaking sobs that night. The kind that come from somewhere ancient. But I stayed. I didn't numb. I didn't escape. I didn't disappear.

I don't remember if I prayed—but I'm sure I did. Just reaching for something. For Him. Even though I didn't really know Him yet.

That night taught me something I wouldn't understand until much later: early sobriety isn't about healing. It's about learning how to stay.

I was still choosing familiar patterns. Still drawn to what mirrored my wounds. Still confused about love. Triangles felt familiar because love had always required competition. Somewhere early on, my body learned that closeness meant waiting, proving, hoping to be chosen. And that ache felt like home.

But something inside me was changing anyway—quietly, without language.

Even in heartbreak. Even in confusion. Even inside old patterns. I stayed. I didn't drink. I didn't disappear.

Gaslighting. Manipulation. Subtle control. The kind that doesn't leave bruises but leaves you doubting your own reality. The kind that makes you feel dramatic for reacting—even while your body is screaming *no*. He was very good at it. And that scared me, even if I couldn't articulate why.

It was familiar in the most dangerous way.

I had been trained my whole life to override my discomfort, to explain it away, to stay polite, to stay small. So, instead of trusting what I felt, I questioned myself. Again.

But my body never did.

What I understand now is that fear doesn't always look like panic. Sometimes, it looks like dread. Like exhaustion. Like wanting to disappear from a room without knowing why. And I hated how it felt—because somewhere deep down I knew this wasn't love. This was survival dressed up as connection.

I didn't abandon myself. And that was the beginning.

That season didn't end cleanly.

After I moved out and found a little house in Derby, I thought I was finally creating distance. Space. Safety. But he didn't disappear. He came back—not in a romantic way, not even clearly; just there. Showing up. Calling. Calling again. Dropping by. Hovering.

And something in my body hated it.

I didn't have words for why yet. I just knew I felt unsettled every time I saw his name on my phone. My stomach would drop. My chest would tighten. I felt small again. Off balance. On edge. And I remember thinking, *Why does this feel so bad if nothing "bad" is happening?*

Now I know.

That was my nervous system responding to emotional abuse.

And still—because life is never just one thing—something beautiful came out of that relationship.

His daughter. And I loved her. She was special to me. Smart. Funny. Grounded in a way that made me laugh. At one point, she was even my roommate, and we shared real life together—conversations, inside jokes, late-night talks.

She was one of the first people I told about the guy I'd met at The Boulevard. She stood in my wedding when I married that guy. There's always a blessing in the heart of things—even the hard ones.

That season taught me something essential: not all harm is loud, and not all lessons come without grace. Sometimes, the body learns first. Sometimes, the blessing and the warning exist side by side. And sometimes, the most important thing you can do is listen—even when you don't yet understand what your body is trying to protect you from.

That understanding would come later.

For now, I was still learning how to leave.

How to choose differently.

How to trust myself—one shaky step at a time.

I met Caleb—at least, that's what I'll call him—in a way that's hard to explain—like something that felt small in the moment but somehow stayed. One interaction, and then suddenly, he was part of my life. He walked into The Boulevard, where I managed the venue, and I swear something inside me sat up and paid attention.

He was cute—soft-eyed, simple, and the kind of quiet that felt safe. We didn't say much that day, just a few words, but I remember thinking he was so cute—something about him just drew me in. I walked away smiling, a little giddy, like I'd just stepped into something I didn't fully understand yet. I didn't question it. Something in me just… picked him.

I helped him with what he needed for the chillers that day. We barely talked—maybe ten words total—but it didn't matter.

I walked back into the office, looked at my friend, and said, "I'm going to marry him." I have no explanation other than God—or maybe my inner child—nodded at the same time.

Our first date was at Carrabba's Italian. A booth, two introverts, trying. No fireworks conversation. No movie-style spark. Just the feeling of being chosen—finally chosen—by someone gentle. Before we even backed out of my driveway that night, he said he needed to blow into the device installed in his truck from a DUI. You'd think that would've stopped me or scared me. It didn't even scratch the surface. I was so wrapped up in hope that red flags looked like confetti. At thirty-five, fresh out of rehab, barely discovering who I was, I didn't know what a red flag even was.

That first night at Carrabba's was also the only time I can remember us ever sitting across from each other. A booth. Face to face. Two people learning about each other in the open space between us. After that, he always sat beside me—never across. In boats, in restaurants, anywhere there was a choice, he chose next to me.

At the time, I loved it. It felt intimate, protective, endearing. Like he wanted to be close enough to touch me, close enough to feel connected without distance. I smiled about it for years. It became one of those small things I carried as proof of tenderness.

Only later—after healing, after language, after the slow unraveling—I wondered if that closeness also spared him something. Conversation. Eye contact. The vulnerability of sitting face to face and being fully seen.

I don't know if that was conscious or instinctive. I don't even know if it matters. What I know is this: the only time we ever sat across from each other was the very beginning.

And somehow, that feels like a truth I couldn't see yet—but my body remembered. I just smiled, told him it was fine, and thought, *Wow... what an adventure.*

We were two quiet people trying to fit into each other's worlds. I mistook his silence for wisdom, his emotional fragility for softness, and his lack of words for humility. Now, I understand it differently. But back then, vulnerability and love looked the same to me. Maybe it was innocence. Maybe it was survival. Maybe it was God. Probably all three.

When we started to hang out, I was infatuated—plain and simple. He felt safe in a way that my nervous system clung to without question. After a lifetime of chaos, inconsistency, alcoholism, and emotional starvation, he was steady. Predictable. Good. Quiet in a way that didn't hurt me.

I confused stillness with safety. I confused a lack of communication with peace, and emotional limitation with gentleness. But at the time, it felt like everything I had ever wanted.

He gave me what I had longed for my whole life: the feeling of being chosen. I had searched for men to fill that hole for years, mostly in the wrong places, mostly through addiction and abandonment patterns. But this time felt different. He felt like the opposite of chaos

The proposal is one of the sweetest memories of my life. I was in the brown recliner when the garage door opened. He walked in with his two boys, five and eight at the time. Each knelt in front of my chair with a Gerber daisy, my favorite.

Three daisies. Three boys. Three little hearts asking me to join theirs. He said, "We want to know if you'll be part of the rest of our lives."

I said yes through tears—the kind that come from a girl who'd never felt chosen before. I was giddy, overwhelmed, but certain. I didn't hesitate. In that moment, I felt loved, seen, wanted, picked. A prayer I didn't even know I had prayed had been answered.

I've always known I wanted to be a mother. Not a question. Not a wish. A calling. In high school, while other girls wrote about careers, I wrote: *I want to be a mom.*

So, one night, sitting on the couch, I told him, "I want a baby. I don't know where you are with that, but I need to know because I'm going to have one."

There was something about him that softened me. Maybe it was the calm. Maybe it was the little boy inside him, though I didn't have language for that until years later. But in those first years, it felt safe—or close enough to safety that my nervous system accepted it as the best it had ever known.

Our early rhythm was sweet. Dinners, laughter, and an intimacy that was fun and exciting. I remember once saying to him, "Isn't this so exciting? We can have sex whenever we want and it's okay!"—like that was maturity, like little Tammy inside me was celebrating freedom.

We were two quiet people trying to learn each other, and in the way new love often does, we filled in the blanks with hope. The silence always lived between us, even at the beginning. I see that now. A stillness that never grew, never deepened. Back then, I translated it as peace. As gentleness. As safety. I had never known love without chaos, so quiet felt like heaven.

I think I fell in love for the first time at thirty-five. That still shocks me to say.

When I imagined our future, I imagined growth. Shared depth. Layers unfolding as we learned each other. I thought we would talk more with time—be open, be vulnerable, become a team. I thought we would build something emotional together, not just live beside each other.

And honestly? I thought being chosen meant being loved. I didn't know yet that they aren't the same.

Becoming a Mother—The Dream That Named Me

I didn't have a detailed picture of motherhood. I just knew I was born for it. That calling lived in my bones long before I knew God. When we decided to have a baby, everything inside me lit up.

Pregnancy was happy for me—even when it was hard. I truly loved being pregnant. But I'll never forget the moment I found out I had gestational diabetes.

I had just pulled into work downtown when the doctor's office called to tell me I'd failed the test. My heart dropped. I started crying right there in the car, confused and scared.

The nurse reassured me that it wasn't anything I had done—that sometimes, it just happens. But all I could think was that I was responsible for this life inside of me. Even with her reassurance, I still felt like it was my fault.

Yet a few months later, there she was, six pounds nine ounces—perfect. Not too big, like I'd feared. Just right. She was the most beautiful thing I had ever seen—both in my arms and in my body.

A quiet whisper inside me said, *You're okay—you can do this.*

It happened after she was born. We were living in the log cabin—such a sacred, simple time—and one night, we disagreed about where Maddie should sleep. I thought she should be close. I wanted her near us. But Caleb said the bassinet shouldn't be in our room, so it wasn't.

I didn't argue. I didn't ask again. I listened to the way my body had been trained since childhood—keep the peace, don't upset anyone, don't create conflict.

So, Maddie slept in another room. Not because I believed it was best—but because he did. Looking back, that was the first time I swallowed myself to keep us calm.

It was the first time I felt resistance inside my chest—that quiet little spark that whispered, *This doesn't feel right*. But I ignored it. I was conditioned for that. I had a lifetime of being shaped to appease, adjust, avoid conflict. I loved being a mother so much, I would've walked through fire barefoot just to protect that feeling, and I think I believed keeping things easy was the way to do that.

I did everything. Night feeds. Diaper changes. All the newborn exhaustion. When he told me he couldn't change diapers because he'd gag, that was it. End of story. There wasn't a discussion. There wasn't problem-solving. There wasn't compromise. He said it once, and my nervous system accepted it as law. Conditioned little Tammy inside me nodded and carried the weight quietly.

I didn't ask if we could switch nights. I didn't explain how exhausted I was. I didn't say, "I need help." Because I didn't know how.

New motherhood softened me in the most sacred way. Breastfeeding Maddie—fifteen months; longer than I ever expected—was one of the most meaningful experiences of my life. I remember praying I was doing it right, holding her in the quiet hours when the world was asleep, just me and her and the hum of the night. That season was tender. Holy, even. But that's also when the silence started to hurt.

New motherhood softened me in the most sacred way. It was one of the most meaningful, exhausting, and beautiful experiences of my life.

My survival pathways—the ones my childhood wrote in permanent ink—were stronger than any new instinct I had as a mother. The part of me that wanted change was young, unpracticed, and shaky. But the part trained to appease was seasoned, steady, and loud. So, I stayed quiet.

We didn't fight. That's the confusing part. It wasn't war—it was absence. It was decisions that were never shared. It was needs that I never voiced, because I didn't know I was allowed to have them. He didn't scream. He didn't demand. He just didn't ask. Didn't notice. Didn't reach toward me unless I asked first.

When I did ask for help, he'd give it. But only because the words left my mouth. There was never a moment when he anticipated, noticed, stepped in, or validated me without prompting. And that's what slowly began to ache.

I didn't confide in anyone. Not really. I tried with my mother a couple times, but there was no safety there. No reflection. No guidance. No seeing. So, I did what I had always done—I held it. I swallowed needs. I shaped myself around someone else's comfort. And I didn't realize how much of me went missing.

CHAPTER 5

The Invisible Inheritance

There was something going on underneath all of it that I didn't understand yet.

I loved my daughter. That part was never in question. She was a gift, and I felt that in every way. I showed up for her. I took care of her. I did everything I knew to do.

But there was a quiet confusion underneath it all.

I knew how to meet her physical needs. I fed her, changed her, held her, made sure she was okay. I breastfed her for over a year, and in many ways, it was one of the most meaningful things I've ever done.

But even in that, I felt like I was following what I thought I was supposed to do more than actually understanding it.

I remember how structured everything felt. Her naps, her bedtime—everything had to happen at certain times. I kept her on a schedule without ever really questioning it. I just assumed that's what you do. That's what a good mom does.

I didn't know why. I didn't understand the reasoning behind it. I just followed it. I did that with a lot of things.

Decisions I made for her, for myself—I didn't research, I didn't question, and I didn't stop to ask what felt right. I just did what I thought I was supposed to do.

That's how I had learned to move through life.

Even when I felt unsure, I didn't slow down and sit with it. I moved forward and told myself I would figure it out later.

There were moments I couldn't explain. Times I felt unsure, even when nothing was technically wrong. Moments when I felt like I should know what to do or how to feel—but didn't. I didn't question it. I assumed I would grow into it.

I remember wanting her close to me. It felt natural, like that's where she belonged. But when that didn't happen, I didn't push it. I didn't ask again. I told myself it was fine.

There were small moments like that—where something in me paused for a second, but I moved past it and kept going.

As she got a little older, I started taking care of myself more. I paid attention to my health. I worked on my body. I tried to become stronger, steadier, better. But even then, there was still something I didn't fully understand.

It wasn't obvious. It wasn't loud. It was just there—this quiet disconnect I couldn't name. I didn't see it as a problem. I saw it as something I needed to get better at. So, I kept going the only way I knew how. I adjusted, stayed quiet, and made things work.

I learned how to pay attention to everyone else's emotions before my own—how to sense what was needed before anything was said; how to soften, shift, and keep things steady. By then, that part of me was automatic.

It didn't feel like I was losing myself. It felt like I was doing what I was supposed to do. I thought I was doing it right.

I thought exhaustion was just part of motherhood. I thought feeling emotionally alone was normal. I thought constantly managing everyone else's emotions was just what good women did.

And the truth is, I loved being her mom. I really did. Some of my favorite memories still come from those years when Maddie was little. We had so much fun together. I loved taking care of her, making things special, and trying to get everything "right."

What I didn't understand then was how much children absorb. They absorb your patterns, your language, your nervous system, and your way of moving through the world. (That alone could be an entire book.)

I didn't realize how much of myself she was learning, simply by watching me survive.

PART TWO

SURVIVAL SEASONS

CHAPTER 6

Becoming the Caretaker

Somewhere along the way, I stopped questioning how I showed up in the world.

It didn't happen all at once. It wasn't a decision I made. It was something that had already been forming for a long time—and by this point, it felt normal.

Motherhood didn't create it, but it revealed it. The way I stayed quiet. The way I adjusted. The way I focused on what everyone else needed before I ever stopped to ask what I needed.

I didn't see it as a pattern. I saw it as who I was. And over time, that way of being followed me into everything.

Caretaking wasn't something I thought about—it was just how I moved through the world. It showed up everywhere—in my relationships, in the way I loved, in the way I gave, and in how I stayed longer than I should have.

I didn't know how to just be with people. I only knew how to take care of them. And for a long time, I thought that was the same thing as love.

In relationships, that looked like overgiving—again and again—until I was exhausted and didn't understand why.

I became a people pleaser without realizing it. Not because I was weak, but because, somewhere deep inside, I believed that being easy to love meant being less likely to be rejected.

I tolerated things I shouldn't have—disrespect, confusion, and people who didn't have good intentions. Not because I thought I deserved it, but because it felt familiar.

And familiar, at the time, felt like safety.

After rehab, I went right back into it. Getting sober changed my drinking—but it didn't change my patterns.

I didn't have the language yet for what I was doing. I didn't understand trauma or nervous system wiring or any of it. I just knew how to function the only way I ever had.

So, I took care of people.

I remember being in relationships where I gave everything and still felt like I wasn't chosen—like I was standing just outside of something I couldn't quite reach.

And instead of walking away, I tried harder. Gave more. Adjusted more. Stayed longer. Because that's what I knew.

Now I can see how deeply this was wired in me. Caretaking wasn't just something I did—it was something that had been formed in me over time.

It made me feel useful. It made me feel connected. It made me feel safe.

And underneath all of it, there was still a part of me that didn't know how to exist without earning my place in someone else's life. But I didn't recognize it then. I didn't think anything was wrong. It just felt like how life worked.

I didn't feel homesick, because I didn't know there was something to miss. I didn't even realize something was missing.

It wasn't until years later, sitting in a therapy room, that things started to make sense. That was the first time I was introduced to something called Complex PTSD.

I had heard of PTSD before. I think most people have. But what I didn't understand then was that complex PTSD doesn't come from one moment.

It comes from living inside something over time—environments where your nervous system never fully settles, where safety is inconsistent, and where love and pain become intertwined. And without your realizing it, it begins to shape how you see yourself, how you attach, and how you survive.

At the time, I didn't have language for any of this. I just knew I was tired—deep in my bones—and I didn't understand why.

I will share more about this later, as I began to understand it myself. But this was the beginning of seeing my life through a different lens.

The version of me people responded to most was the one who did everything for everyone else—always before myself. People didn't ask how I was, and if they did, it wasn't a real question.

At the time, I didn't feel exhausted. This was normal for me. It was a well-worn path I didn't know how to step off of. But I was running on fumes—body, mind, and soul—for years. I thought this level of exhaustion and confusion was normal.

This is where the caretaker was formed—not out of choice, but out of survival.

CHAPTER 7

The House on Topeka Street

There was an incident that happened when I was a little girl. It's not something I'm going to describe in detail. But it changed me, and my body carried it for years.

I've learned there are places your body remembers before your mind ever fully understands. The house on Topeka Street is one of those places for me.

I don't remember everything clearly—not in a way that forms a clean story. But I do remember how it felt, how people reacted, and how I was made to feel.

I didn't have language for it then. I didn't understand what was happening or why. I just knew, instinctively, to be quiet. To not move. To not make it worse.

In that stillness, my body learned something it would carry for a long time—how to survive without being seen.

I didn't talk about it. Not then. Not for years. In many ways, I carried it quietly for most of my life.

And it wasn't just what happened. It was everything that came after. The little girl who had been hurt was the one who carried the shame.

She was blamed. Dismissed. Left to make sense of something she never should have had to carry alone. No one told her it wasn't her fault. In fact, the opposite was implied.

That's the kind of damage I'm talking about—not just the moment itself, but the aftermath.

When a child isn't told the truth about what happened to them, they create their own. And most of the time, that truth sounds like: *this was my fault.*

So, she learned to hold it tightly. To bury it. To keep going like nothing had happened.

And for years, that's exactly what I did.

I'm not going to unpack all of it here. I don't have to. I get to choose how I tell my story.

But it matters that you know it happened—because it shaped more of my life than I understood for a very long time.

It wasn't until nearly thirty years later, sitting in a therapist's office, trying to put words to something I had never spoken out loud, that I began to understand the weight of what I had been carrying.

This is something I didn't understand for a long time. I'll come back to it.

CHAPTER 8

When Survival Became Responsibility

By that point, nothing I was doing felt unusual.

The way I moved through relationships, the way I showed up for people, the way I adjusted without thinking—it all felt normal to me. I didn't question it, because I had never known anything different.

I wasn't aware of patterns. I wasn't aware of trauma. I didn't have language for what was happening inside of me.

I just knew how to function.

I had a lot of different jobs during that time, but one that stands out most was when I worked at a title company. I was an administrative assistant, and at the time, I thought I was doing well. I showed up, I worked hard, and I did what was expected of me.

But looking back now, there was a lot happening in that environment that I didn't fully understand.

My boss struggled with addiction. The office itself felt chaotic in a quiet way—there was always gossip, tension, things being said behind people's backs. It was the kind of place where you could feel something was off, but no one really said it out loud.

I didn't have the awareness to name any of it. I just stayed in my role and kept going.

There were moments that should have stood out more to me than they did. I remember having to tell my boss more than once that I wasn't interested in anything inappropriate. At the time, I said no, but I didn't fully recognize how wrong it was that I had to say it at all. I didn't question the environment. I didn't step back and ask why that dynamic existed. I just handled it and moved on.

That was a pattern for me.

It wasn't just there. I started to notice that a lot of the authority figures in my life—especially men—carried a certain tone. Like they had permission to say things, to comment, or to cross lines in subtle ways. And I didn't challenge it. I adjusted around it.

I remember tension with other women in the office. There was one woman in marketing who always carried herself like she was above everyone else. Whether that was actually true or not didn't matter—what I felt was the pressure of it. I didn't know how to navigate those dynamics, either. I just stayed in my lane and tried to keep things smooth.

Around that time, alcohol started becoming more present in my life, too. It didn't feel like a problem then. It just slowly became part of how I coped, how I socialized, and how I got through things I didn't fully understand.

That was the season when I got my DUI.

I remember how much that disrupted my life, but what stands out even more is my friend, Lesa. She showed up for me in a way I didn't expect. Every day, while my license was suspended, she came by to pick me up and take me to work. I paid her gas money, but she didn't have to do that for me. She chose to.

I remember how much that meant to me. How seen I felt by that kind of consistency and care. That's the part that stayed with me.

But even then, I didn't zoom out and look at the bigger picture of my life. I didn't connect the dots between my environment, my choices, and what I was carrying internally.

At the time, I mistook familiarity for safety. I didn't yet understand that something feeling familiar didn't automatically make it healthy.

So, I kept moving forward the only way I knew how.

PART THREE

THE UNRAVELING

CHAPTER 9

The Duplex Years

The duplex.

Even saying those words now makes my chest tighten.

I didn't understand that feeling then. I didn't know how to listen to my body or what it was trying to tell me. I just kept moving, like I always had. But now, I can see it clearly—something about that time in my life sits differently inside of me.

This part of my life feels different in my body than anything else. Heavier. Darker.

The duplex years weren't just a time in my life. They were a state. A dissociated one.

A holding place for pain I didn't yet know how to name.

Here's the part that still blows my mind.

My mom and my dad lived in that duplex when I was a baby. I have pictures of my mom standing in that kitchen, giving me a bath, when I was maybe six months old. That same kitchen. That same space.

And decades later, I chose to live there again.

Though at the time I didn't realize it, my body had circled back to something unfinished. I'd returned to the place where my nervous system first learned survival—and stayed there far too long.

I lived in that duplex for years. I paid my mother rent to live there. Years of my twenties and early thirties passed inside those walls. And those years were filled with addiction, dissociation, codependency, and more pain than I had words for at the time.

But the duplex holds more than just darkness, when I look back on it now. I can still see the cement walls. I can still picture the driveway and the ramps that led to the backyard—the ones built by my dad and his brother, Ray, whom I knew as my dad my whole life. There's so much history in that place. So many layers. So many versions of me.

There were good moments, too. That's what makes it complicated.

There were good moments there, too. A lot of them, actually. We had parties at the duplex—Halloween costumes, music playing, people filling the space. I remember dressing up as a biker one year, sitting out on the patio with my friend, Kerri after long nights at the Lamplighter, playing pool, laughing, trying to feel free for a little while.

There were moments when I truly felt connected, like maybe I belonged somewhere. But underneath all of it, there was still a sadness and confusion in me I didn't fully understand yet.

Because underneath all of that… I was not okay.

The duplex held my secrets.

It held the mornings I woke up already exhausted with myself. Standing in front of the mirror, promising—today will be different. Today, I'll change. Today, I won't drink like that again.

And then… I did.

Over and over and over again.

Wine was my thing. The thick, dark-red bottles—not the cute skinny ones. I could down half a bottle without blinking. And if it wasn't wine, it was Jack Daniels. Not a little bottle. A fifth. Easily.

And then came the shame. The self-hatred. The confusion. The why-can't-I-stop spiral.

I hated myself for what I was doing. And I hated myself even more because I couldn't stop.

Everything was tangled—the alcohol, the trauma, my relationship with my mother, my inability to feel safe or grounded. I hadn't touched any of it. Not even close.

I was numbing what I didn't know how to survive.

And one of the moments that stays with me the most is Chloe. My boxer. My girl.

I remember pulling into the duplex driveway with my mom. My boyfriend at the time had called—something had happened, but I didn't fully understand what. When we got there, Chloe was in the backseat of my car, and he was getting ready to take her to the vet.

She was already gone.

I don't even know how to explain that moment fully, because part of me still doesn't understand what happened. But I remember the feeling. I remember how disoriented I was. How quickly everything shifted.

I had been gone, trying to get better, trying to get sober, trying to come back different… and instead, I came back to loss.

I remember bawling my eyes out. Not the kind of crying you can control—but the kind that takes over your whole body. I didn't know what to do with it. I didn't know where to put that kind of pain. My chest hurt. My body felt heavy and shaky all at the same time. I just remember crying and crying, completely overwhelmed, completely heartbroken.

And instead of being met with comfort or space to grieve, everything around me felt tense. Loud. Chaotic. There was anger. Yelling. Conflict.

I didn't feel safe in my grief.

I just remember crying and feeling completely alone in it.

And at some point, my mom didn't know what to do with me. I was too emotional. Too upset. Too much for that moment. So, she took me to my doctor—Dr. M, who had been our doctor for years, since I was a little girl.

I remember being brought into that office still crying, still completely undone. I wasn't calm. I wasn't composed. I was raw. My whole body felt like it was vibrating with grief and shock and confusion.

I realize now I wasn't trying to be fixed—I was heartbroken. I think I just needed someone to sit with me in it. To see me. To let me cry, feel, and release what my body was carrying. But that wasn't something we knew how to do then. So instead, I was taken somewhere to be managed, when really, I was just grieving.

But that wasn't something we knew how to do.

So instead, I was taken somewhere to be managed… when really, I was just heartbroken.

Losing her. Standing in that driveway. Being in that car. And then, being pulled right back into everything else that was already breaking me.

That's what it felt like living there.

Like being already wounded—raw and hurting—and then, having that wound pressed on again and again. Not once. Not twice. But over and over.

It wasn't just, "I hurt you and I'm sorry."

It was, "I hurt you… and I keep hurting you."

That was the environment. That was the pattern.

And what's hard to admit is… that feeling didn't just live there. I've felt that same kind of pain in other seasons of my life.

The duplex years weren't just about the drinking. They were also about the way I clung to men—looking for something I didn't even have language for yet. I thought I was looking for love, but really, I was looking for safety. For someone to choose me. To stay. To make me feel like I mattered.

I had no measuring stick for what love was supposed to look like. None. I didn't know what was healthy. I didn't know what was safe. And I definitely didn't know what I deserved. So, I accepted whatever felt close enough, even when it wasn't good for me. Even when it hurt.

When I left, I carried a clarity I had never felt before. It wasn't loud or dramatic, but it was steady and certain: I could not go back to the duplex. I knew it in my body. I knew it in my bones. Going back there meant slipping right back into everything that had been destroying me.

But knowing that didn't make it easy.

I remember crying, trying to explain to my mom. Trying to put words to something that felt so clear inside me but seemed impossible to communicate. We fought. We yelled. It was emotional and exhausting, and underneath all of it was this quiet truth I couldn't ignore: if I went back into that space, I would not survive.

I knew it in my bones.

The duplex had become something else entirely in my mind. It didn't feel like a home anymore—it felt like a place my body associated with destruction. Like a black hole I had barely made it out of.

I knew that going back there wouldn't just be uncomfortable—it would pull me right back into everything I had fought so hard to leave behind.

But that truth didn't land gently.

The fight with my mom was intense. Our relationship had already been strained for years, but this cracked something open in a way that felt irreversible. I had just done one of the hardest things of my life—I had gotten sober. I had chosen something different for myself.

And instead of being met with understanding or even a moment of recognition… I was met with anger. With resistance. With blame.

I remember thinking, *How could she not be proud of me?*

I was sober. I had chosen recovery. And still, I was being yelled at. Still being told I was the problem. Still being torn down at a time when I was trying so hard to hold myself together.

It was disorienting. Painful in a way that's hard to explain, unless you've lived it—being at your most vulnerable and still not feeling safe. It shook my nervous system to its core.

But before that, before the recovery center, there was one night in the duplex I will never forget.

I was alone in that living room, on the green couch—the one that had seen the worst of me.

I remember lying there, so sick. Physically, mentally, completely broken.

There are moments in addiction that stay with you—not because they were dramatic, but because of how deeply you felt them in your body. That couch was one of those moments for me.

I remember feeling so awful there. So many times.

Something about that space held it all.

And something inside me surrendered.

It wasn't a loud moment. It wasn't dramatic. It was quiet. But it was real.

Leaving the recovery center should have felt like a beginning. In some ways, it was. But it also marked another rupture. Another moment where I needed safety and didn't feel it.

The tension with my mom didn't resolve—it deepened. What could have been a turning point became another layer of confusion, another reminder of how unstable things still felt.

After the duplex, I moved in with friends for a while, trying to find some sense of normalcy. Eventually, I made my way to Derby—toward something that felt like a different life, even if I didn't fully know what that meant yet.

But the duplex years didn't just stay behind me.

I didn't talk about what I had been through. Not really. I kept it in, learned how to carry it quietly, like that was just what you were supposed to do.

The more I held in, though, the heavier it got. The pain didn't go away—it just settled deeper. And without even realizing it, silence became part of how I survived.

And my body paid for it.

My pancreatitis began in those years—directly tied to alcohol. My body was screaming long before my mind understood why.

I can see now what that place was doing to me.

The duplex wasn't just where I lived.

It was where I disappeared.

And it was where the first whisper of surrender finally broke through.

What the duplex gave me was survival. What it cost me was myself.

Silence kept me alive back then. Dissociation protected me when I didn't have the tools to feel, name, or escape what I was drowning in. It helped me endure addiction, rejection, and pain that would have broken me otherwise. But it also kept me stuck—frozen in patterns that taught my body to disappear instead of ask for help.

I don't shame that version of me anymore. She did the best she could with what she had. But the truth is this: staying quiet saved me then—and nearly destroyed me later. And eventually, my body would stop agreeing to that arrangement.

The duplex was where I learned to numb. And it was also where surrender quietly began for me.

CHAPTER 10

Pancreatitis & the Body's Alarm

There was a moment when my body didn't just whisper anymore… it screamed. And this time, it wasn't the first warning. It was one I couldn't ignore.

Christmas Eve, 2015.

My mom and I had just gotten back from my cousins' house. We hadn't spent the holidays with that side of the family in a couple of years, and it meant so much to be there again. I loved them deeply. The night felt warm and familiar—the kind of holiday evening you don't want to end. And the food was everything it had always been. Homemade, comforting, and yes—greasy. We enjoyed it fully. Maybe a little too fully.

We got home around 10 p.m. My husband was already in bed, asleep. Maddie was asleep too. The house was quiet in that still, dim, Christmas Eve kind of way.

At first, it just felt like a stomach ache. But it didn't stay that way.

It got worse. And worse. Until I was doubled over on the living room floor, curled into myself, trying to breathe through something that wouldn't let up. I remember gripping the carpet, my body tense, my chest feeling tight and strange.

I kept trying to reason with it. It's just my stomach. I'll go to the bathroom, and I'll feel better. I sat in there for a while, waiting for relief that never came.

And then came the familiar pattern. I started questioning myself.

What if I'm overreacting?

What if it's not that bad?

I can push through this.

I walked into the bedroom more than once. He was sound asleep. I stood there for a moment, trying to decide if I should say something… and then I'd walk back out.

Because, at that time, a part of me believed it was easier to endure the pain than to speak up.

I went back and forth like that for what felt like an hour—lying on the living room floor, getting up, going to the bedroom, turning around, second-guessing myself again.

Until I couldn't do it anymore.

I walked in and said, "Hey babe…"

He turned over.

"I'm hurting really bad. I think I'm going to go to the ER."

Even as I said it, I questioned it. "I don't know… maybe I'm overreacting."

I walked back out again, still hoping it would pass.

It didn't. So, I called my mom.

I was crying when she answered. I could barely get the words out, but she didn't hesitate. She came to get me and took me to the ER.

We waited for what felt like forever. The pain kept escalating—sharp, consuming, breath-stealing—until eventually they hooked me up to morphine. And for the first time all night, I could finally breathe.

Pancreatitis. Again.

I remember lying there in disbelief. I hadn't had a drop of alcohol in five years. I had done the work. I truly believed that part of my life was behind me for good.

But this time, it had nothing to do with alcohol. It was food...

Greasy food. Processed food. Convenience. Everything I had normalized without realizing the impact it was still having on my body. I didn't know my body could break like that again. I didn't know it was still keeping score.

They also found a cyst sitting right against my pancreas that needed to be removed. I remember feeling shocked—trying to make sense of how all of this was happening.

I stayed overnight, and while so much of it felt like a blur—the exhaustion, the fear, the confusion—there's one moment I remember so clearly.

My husband brought all three kids up to see me. Our boys and my baby girl, standing there in the doorway of my hospital room.

I was so happy to see them. So relieved. Something in me softened in that moment, like, Momma is okay... Momma is here... and I get to go home soon. That moment stayed with me.

Writing this now, ten years later, I didn't expect to feel this emotional—but I do. Because I can see her so clearly. Curled up on that living room floor, in pain, trying to convince herself she was fine. Trying to endure instead of asking for help.

And I feel so much compassion for her. No shame. Just understanding.

She didn't know.

But I also see how far I've come. Because today, that wouldn't be an option anymore. I wouldn't lay there for an hour, questioning whether I was "allowed" to get help. I wouldn't try to endure something my body was clearly telling me needed attention.

That hospital stay cracked something open in me.

For the first time, I couldn't explain it away as bad luck or timing. Something in me knew: I couldn't keep living this way.

And I listened—at least partially.

By March 2016, I made a decision that I would never feel that kind of physical pain again if I could help it. I started changing how I ate. I started creating new habits. I found structure. Discipline. Control. I found something that worked—and my body responded quickly. The weight dropped. My energy came back. I felt strong again.

And in many ways, it was a turning point.

But what I didn't realize at the time was this: I was healing my body without touching my trauma. I was changing my habits without changing my patterns. I was building discipline on top of survival.

All I really knew at the time was that the pain scared me straight. And fear has always been a powerful motivator for me. So, I did what I knew how to do.

I got serious.

I got focused.

I got "healthy."

I told myself I was choosing life—and in a lot of ways, I was.

But I was also choosing control. Control felt safer than uncertainty. Structure felt safer than rest. Discipline felt safer than slowing down and asking harder questions about why my body had broken down in the first place.

If I followed the rules, I believed I could avoid pain. If I stayed consistent, nothing could blindside me again. If I stayed ahead of my body, I wouldn't have to listen so closely.

I didn't think of it that way then. I just thought I was being strong. And everyone around me agreed.

As my routines became more consistent, people started noticing. And not just people I knew—strangers, too. I received so many messages from people thanking me for showing up, for sharing honestly, and for inspiring them through my stories. And it did something to me. For the first time in a long time, I felt like I was actually good at something. I genuinely loved connecting with people in that way.

It felt so good—almost unfamiliar—to be seen like that. To be told I was doing something right. More than that… that I was helping people. The more it happened, the more I started to believe maybe I really was good at this. That maybe I had finally found something I could not only succeed at—but genuinely enjoy.

I wasn't used to that kind of affirmation. Kindness like that felt new. And I held onto it.

The more it happened, the more I started to believe it. That maybe I really was good at this. That maybe I had finally found something I could get right.

It felt better to be admired than to be afraid. It felt better to feel successful than to feel vulnerable. It felt better to believe I was "fixed" than to ask what had actually been breaking me all along.

I was rebuilding myself from the outside in. And for a while, it worked.

But no amount of clean eating taught my nervous system how to feel safe. No routine taught me how to rest. No discipline touched the grief my body had been holding for years.

I was taking care of my body the same way I had always taken care of everyone else—with intensity, vigilance, and very little softness.

Even healing became something I felt like I needed to do well. Like it was something to achieve… instead of something to feel.

CHAPTER 11

When Strength Looked Like Success

After my hospitalization, I made a vow. I didn't know how to heal emotionally yet, but I knew I had to do *something* for my health. So, I decided to start a new fitness and nutrition rhythm—not a program, not a platform, just a commitment to move my body and nourish it differently.

Maddie was about two and a half, and we started together in the living room. Thirty minutes at a time. Dancing. Laughing. Moving. I dropped twelve or thirteen pounds in twenty-one days. Inches fell off. My energy came back fast—almost shockingly fast. It felt like night and day compared to the months before.

My daughter and I had the best time. It felt joyful. Alive. Easy in a way my life hadn't felt in a long time.

My body started changing, and people noticed. I shared online—and the overwhelming response surprised me. It felt like love. Encouragement. Being seen in a way that felt new. And something inside me exhaled.

I didn't know it then, but that moment mattered more than the weight loss.

I joined an online challenge group, and those first few months were pure magic. I had never experienced support like that before. I was cheered on. Loved exactly where I was. Allowed to show up messy. Allowed to screw up. Allowed to be human. It felt revolutionary. And years later—long after I left that business—I finally understood why I stayed for so long.

When I first started implementing new habits, it felt like everything shifted almost overnight. Some days, I would get my workout in while she napped. Other days, she was right there with me—on the living room floor, trying to copy my movements, asking questions, being part of it. It became our thing.

There were so many new pieces I was learning—meal prepping, supplements, routines that actually made me feel better instead of depleted. And within the first ten days, I felt it. A real shift. My energy came back in a way that almost didn't make sense after how I had been feeling for so long. By the end of the first few weeks, my body was changing quickly, but more than that, I felt alive again.

So, I kept going.

After the first month, I didn't even question it. Why would I stop? I felt good. I loved how I felt. And naturally, I started helping other women do the same thing. I didn't fully understand the business side of it yet, but I didn't care.

Every morning, I woke up and immediately checked in with my challenge groups. That's what we called them—these online spaces full of women showing up, sharing real life, encouraging each other. I would post my workouts, share what I was eating, talk about what I was learning, and then pour into them the same way they poured into me. It didn't feel like work. It felt like connection. It felt like purpose.

I loved it. Truly.

There was something about being in those groups that felt like a breath of fresh air. For the first time in my life, I felt seen. Heard. Encouraged in a way that didn't feel forced or conditional. Women I had never met were showing up for me, and I was showing up for them. We shared the big things, the small things, and everything in between.

I learned quickly that I loved creating—taking pictures, sharing pieces of my life, connecting through social media. I showed up consistently. Three times a day, sometimes more. Posting, responding, engaging. It became a rhythm. A system. Something I could follow, something I could measure.

And people noticed.

There were comments. Messages. Women reaching out telling me I inspired them, asking how I did it, wanting me to coach them. And then there were the quieter messages—the ones that didn't come with attention, but meant everything. The ones that said, I kept going today because of something you shared. Those were the ones that stayed with me.

It did something inside of me. It filled something I didn't even have language for yet.

Because, on one hand, it felt good—really good—to know I was helping people, to see that what I was doing mattered. But on the other hand, it started to mess with me in ways I couldn't see clearly at the time. People saw me as strong. Disciplined. Motivated. Someone who had figured it out.

And parts of that were true. But parts of it weren't.

They didn't see the pain I was still carrying. The things I hadn't touched. The parts of my life—my heart, my marriage, my past—that were still very much unresolved. And I didn't know how to hold both of those truths at the same time.

So, I kept going.

The structure made sense to me—the consistency, the clear expectations. Post throughout the day. Get your workout in. Stay on plan. Help others do the same. There were goals, deadlines, and recognition. A system I could follow.

And I liked it. It felt like progress. Like validation. Like I was finally doing something right.

What I didn't see then was that something else was forming underneath it—something I wouldn't understand until much later.

But underneath that, something else was happening.

If a workout didn't happen, or my routine got disrupted, I could feel it immediately in my body. Anxiety would rise before I even had a chance to think about it. My mind would start racing—you need to get it in, it doesn't matter what else is going on, just get it done. And even if I told myself I would do it later, there was no real grace in that. Not in my body. Not in my nervous system.

I didn't know how to give myself that. I just pushed through. That's what I had always done.

Looking back now, I can see it so clearly. I was building discipline on top of survival. I was creating patterns that looked healthy on the outside, but underneath, they were being driven by the same wiring I had lived in for years. The same need to perform, to get it right, to stay ahead of the feeling that something might fall apart if I didn't.

And in many ways, I had found something good.

That season gave me so much. It really did—so much confidence, connection, and growth that I didn't even know I needed.

It gave me proof that I could change my life, that I could help other people change theirs. And one of the things I will always carry with me from that time is this:

My daughter was watching. Through all of it—the workouts, the routines, the growth, the mistakes—she was right there. My three-year-old, then four, then five, then six… watching me show up, watching me take care of my body, sometimes right beside me trying to do it too. That part was real. That part mattered. And I will always be grateful for that.

She's watching you become.

It was a beautiful season. But it wasn't the whole story.

Because, while I was building something that looked like strength, I was also reinforcing patterns I didn't yet understand. I was learning how to show up, how to perform, how to push—but I wasn't learning how to slow down, how to feel, or how to heal what was still underneath it all.

I didn't know it then, but I was wiring something deeper. And eventually, my body would make sure I couldn't ignore it anymore.

It was constant. Click. Check. Post. Respond. Repeat.

It felt productive. Efficient. Rewarding. Like I was always moving forward. Always doing something that mattered.

What I didn't understand was how quickly it was imprinting itself into my body—how good I became at it because it mirrored survival so perfectly. Do the thing. Get the result. Stay ahead. Don't stop.

Even now, I'm literally still unlearning parts of that wiring. I still have to remind myself I don't need to document everything to prove it mattered.

There were so many beautiful things about that season—relationships I wouldn't trade, lessons about human woundedness, and growth that mattered. I don't regret it.

I was healthy. Truly.

I was disciplined.

I was growing.

And I was also still surviving.

You were never meant to do this alone.

I didn't know it yet, but God was slowly, patiently restoring my identity—layer by layer—long before I had the language for what was happening. Long before 2022, when the truth about my mother began to surface. Long before 2023, when I finally went no contact and understood how deeply I had been shaped by silence, loyalty, and survival.

Back then, I thought success meant never slowing down.

Now I know better.

It wasn't the workouts. It wasn't the money. It was the feeling of being seen, heard, and encouraged in a way I had never experienced before.

I didn't know it then, but I was starving for support. For affirmation. For community. For someone to see me.

For someone to look at me and say, *I see you. You're doing great. You matter.*

And when I finally felt that—even through a screen—it changed everything.

So, I went all in.

I built a business around health, fitness, and connection, and I loved it. It gave me tools I didn't know I needed. Confidence. Discipline. Momentum. A sense of purpose.

What I didn't realize was that the same perfectionism that kept me showing up was the same survival wiring I'd been carrying since childhood. The part of me that learned early: *If I do it better, if I try harder, if I don't stop—maybe I'll be enough.*

That pathway lit up fast.

That season was a blessing and a curse. It gave my nervous system something it had never had—structure, affirmation, and momentum. And at the same time, it slowly overwhelmed it.

I loved how good I was at it. I hated how much of me it consumed. I didn't like being on my phone all the time. I didn't like taking endless photos.

I'd open my camera roll and feel overwhelmed—thousands of images, proof of how much I was producing, performing, and showing up. And yet… I was so good at it.

That season was really, really good—until it wasn't. It gave me confidence and connection and tools that shaped the woman I am today.

And at the same time, it was feeding parts of me that were still unhealed, still running on survival, still chasing worth through output.

I didn't know how to hold both truths yet. But my body did.

CHAPTER 12

The Day Everything Cracked

By that point in my life, I was sober and trying to rebuild everything from the ground up. I had started my online business and was surrounding myself with women—clients, friendships, connections that felt meaningful at the time. I was learning a lot in that season. About people. About relationships. About myself.

But one day shifted something in me in a way I didn't fully understand at the time—but my body did.

I remember exactly where I was. I was driving through my mom's neighborhood when I got a message from someone I trusted—a friend who was also a client I had supported. Even before I opened it, I could feel it wasn't just a normal text. Something in me knew.

I pulled over on the side of the road to read it. And as I went through her message, line by line, I felt my body go still.

It wasn't one thing—it was everything. A list of things I was supposedly doing wrong. The way I showed up online. The way I ran my business. The way I shared—or didn't share—other people's lives. And then, it got more personal.

She questioned my parenting. Made comments about how I was raising Maddie—even something as simple as taking her shopping. She brought up my relationship with my mom. She crossed into every part of my life.

I sat there in my car, stunned.

I remember thinking, *What is happening right now?*

I felt exposed. Misunderstood. And deeply, deeply hurt.

I drove straight to my mom's house, barely holding it together. I walked inside already crying, trying to explain through tears how much it had affected me. I didn't even have words for all of it—I just knew I was hurting and needed comfort.

But instead of being met with softness, I was met with a question.

She looked at me and said, "Well... did you do those things?"

I remember just staring at her.

I was so caught off guard, I didn't even know how to respond. There were so many different accusations in that message—I didn't even know which one she meant. I wasn't asking to be analyzed. I wasn't asking to be corrected. I was asking to be seen.

And she couldn't meet me there.

I tried to explain. I tried to get her to understand how hurt I was, how confusing it felt to be hit with all of that at once. But she didn't budge. There was no validation. No pause to say, "That must have been hard to receive."

Just more distance.

I left feeling even more alone than when I'd walked in.

I got in my car and started driving, but I couldn't hold it together. I had to pull over again. I remember gripping the steering wheel and sobbing—like it was coming from somewhere deep in my body that had been holding too much for too long. I tried to call a friend, but I could barely get words out.

I eventually made it home, still shaken, still trying to process what had just happened. I walked out to the barn where my husband was, because that's where I always went when I got home. He could tell immediately something was wrong.

I handed him my phone and let him read the message. I didn't need him to fix it. I just needed someone to see me.

And he did.

He reminded me—gently, but clearly—not to internalize everything that had just been thrown at me. That not everything said to me was truth. That sometimes, people project, sometimes they stir things up, and sometimes they don't see clearly.

But more than anything, he was on my side. And I can still feel what that meant in that moment.

Because that day wasn't just about a message. It was about what happened next.

It was about bringing my pain to my mother and realizing, in real time, that she couldn't hold it. That was the moment something in me cracked.

That day activated every old imprint at once. The shame. The dismissal. The familiar ache of bringing pain to someone who could not hold it. This is what nervous system betrayal feels like—not dramatic, not loud, but deeply destabilizing. And that moment mattered, because my body finally refused to keep pretending it was safe when it never had been.

What made that season unbearable wasn't just the betrayal. It was how exhausted I already was. I didn't have excess capacity to absorb another emotional hit. I had been holding myself together for years, quietly managing survival, showing up, performing competence, caretaking other people's emotions, and telling myself this was just what adulthood felt like. So, when that message landed, it didn't hit an open wound—it hit a nervous system that had been running on fumes.

I almost forgot how much else was happening at the same time. I was losing my grandparents. Grandpa Smith first, then Grandma not long after. We weren't deeply close, but loss still leaves a mark, especially when it comes with family tension and the kind of quiet ugliness that shows up when people die—arguments, entitlement, materialism. I remember trying to stay out of it. I ended up with my grandpa's saddle and hat, and even that came with discomfort. Death has a way of revealing people's wounds, and there was already so much bleeding during that season.

I was also letting go of a career I had loved—a DJ music company that had been part of my life for years. It no longer fit. I had started it during active addiction, and when I came back sober, it felt misaligned in a way I couldn't fully explain yet. At the same time, Maddie was little—just a few years old—and all I wanted was to be home with her. I was desperate to build a life that didn't require me to leave her behind.

That's when I found online fitness and nutrition. Maddie and I did those thirty-minute workouts together. She danced to the music while I moved my body back into myself. We prepped meals side by side. I built online groups with women and loved them hard—because I knew what it felt like to be unseen, and I never wanted anyone in my space to feel that way. The business grew quickly. And for the first time in my life, admiration, validation, and visibility wrapped themselves around me in a way that felt intoxicating.

Performance became my nervous system's language for safety. That's why the betrayal hit the way it did. That message didn't just criticize me—it dismantled the fragile structure holding me together. And when I brought my pain to my mother and was met with dismissal instead of care, something inside me cracked.

Earlier betrayals hadn't broken me like this, but this one was different. I had a child now. I had built a life. I had worked too hard to survive to keep pretending this didn't matter. I didn't suddenly get weaker. I just got closer to the truth.

Betrayal hurts differently when your nervous system is already awake. You stop being able to explain it away. You stop being able to override it. That wasn't fragility—that was awareness. My body knew before my mind did that something was no longer safe, and for the first time, I couldn't ignore it.

CHAPTER 13

My Most Sacred Goodbyes

Years later, it happened again—another call, another goodbye. My Uncle Rodney. My biggest, baddest teddy bear.

I will never forget the tone of that day—the atmosphere, the heartbreak, the disbelief. He was my favorite person. The one man in my life who loved me with kindness instead of cruelty. Uncle Rodney wasn't perfect, but he was real. He was loyal. He was the one who cared enough about me to go to anger management because he couldn't stand the way my dad, Ray Floyd, treated his own daughter.

We had heart-to-hearts—the kind that stay with you. I adored him. He was my safety place, my constant, my call-anytime person. Our bond ran deep—soul-deep. From the stories I'd heard, he'd been holding me since the day I was born.

Then, one day, the call came.

A hospital in Michigan.

He'd been in a motorcycle accident.

It was my dad's girlfriend, on the phone. Her voice shook as she spoke.

"He's critical," she said. "They need your permission for surgery. You're listed as his next of kin."

The whole thing felt surreal. I had never even been to Michigan, but his chosen family—his biker brothers and sisters—already knew who I was. They knew me as Tammy, his niece, the one he talked about all the time with pride.

Even now, that realization brings tears to my eyes.

I still can't believe he's gone. I wish he were here. I wish he could see Maddie and me now. He would be the first to remind me that I am capable of anything.

I packed my bag and left the next morning. Maddie was only three or four, and it broke my heart to leave her. But there was no hesitation. I knew I was supposed to go. I felt it in my spirit—this was a sacred assignment.

The entire trip felt unreal, like I was moving through something my body hadn't caught up to yet.

I kept thinking, *How am I the one doing this?*

Flying to Michigan. Making decisions. Walking into a hospital room to see him like that.

And somewhere deep down, underneath the fear and the shock, I knew—this mattered. I didn't have language for it then, but I felt it. I was supposed to be there.

Out of everyone, it was me.

The hospital was within walking distance from my hotel, but the walk felt longer than anything I had ever done. When I stepped off the elevator and into the waiting room, everything in me tightened.

The room was full—his people. Leather jackets. Weathered faces. Men who had lived hard lives and loved him deeply.

Every set of eyes turned toward me at once.

I felt exposed. Small. Like I had just walked into something sacred that I didn't fully know how to stand inside of.

I knew they knew who I was—Rodney had made sure of that. I was his niece. The one he talked about. The one he loved out loud.

But knowing that didn't quiet what was happening in my body.

I felt terrified. Alone. Completely unprepared for what I was about to walk into.

I recognized them immediately. I'd grown up around that kind of loyal love. To me, the biker life always meant brotherhood, protection, and devotion without conditions. That was Uncle Rodney—tough on the outside, tender on the inside.

Seeing him in that hospital bed was truly one of the hardest moments of my life. Cuts. Stitches. A metal brace around his head. Machines breathing for him.

I stayed for several nights. I cried constantly. I called family back home, searching for clarity, but no one could give it to me. The doctors told me his brain damage was irreversible—that even if he survived, he would never truly be Rodney again. I stayed for several nights. I barely slept. I cried more than I spoke.

The days blurred together—hospital lights, quiet conversations, waiting for updates that never felt clear enough.

I had never felt that kind of loneliness before. I was surrounded by people, but none of them were mine. Not in the way I needed.

And still… I was grateful to be there. Grateful that he wasn't alone. Grateful that I got to sit beside him, even in that state.

I didn't understand it fully at the time, but something about being there felt like both an unbearable weight and a quiet honor.

One night, back in my hotel room, I collapsed on the floor and sobbed. I whispered to God, even though I wasn't sure I believed He was listening.

And then, peace came.

I know now—it was Him.

God gave me the knowing that my uncle didn't want to live that way. He had too much life, too much pride, too much soul. Keeping him alive like that would have been a prison.

So, I made the hardest decision of my life.

I told them we would remove the ventilator.

When they asked if I wanted to be there, my answer was immediate. "Yes."

They wheeled him into a quiet room in the basement. I remember the cold. The echo of footsteps. The low hum of machines. Someone turned on soft music.

I held his head in my hands as they prepared to disconnect the ventilator. My tears fell onto his face as I whispered: "I love you so much. I'm so proud of you. Please tell Grandma and Grandpa I said hi."

"You've been my person from the very beginning. Thank you for loving me the way you did."

"Please rest now. Please go in peace. God is wrapping His arms around you."

"I love you forever."

Moments later, a nurse said quietly, "He's gone."

They helped me back to his room. I cried until I felt hollow. My body remembers everything—the weight, the ache, the holiness of that moment.

Letting him go was one of the most excruciating, sacred experiences of my life.

And somehow, it was also a gift.

It was God trusting me with one more goodbye. One more release. One more lesson in letting go of someone I loved deeply.

When I returned home, I was changed.

I was physically present with my husband and my little girl, but emotionally, I was elsewhere—grieving, exhausted, spiritually cracked open. Every sound startled me. Every conversation felt too loud. I couldn't explain it to anyone. I felt like I was standing alone on an island, screaming for help.

That trip changed me forever.

It was also the quiet ending of another chapter—my oldest friendship.

While I was in Michigan, I called my best friend of thirty years, Anna, while I was crying in a hospital parking lot. I needed comfort. Instead, she yelled at me—accusing me of something so small, I can't even remember what it was. What I remember is the sound of her voice. The sting of it. The moment something broke inside of me.

When I came home, it was confirmed. Our thirty-year friendship ended—quietly and painfully. Another loss stacked on top of another goodbye.

This was the moment my soul began to collapse under the weight of everything I had carried. It felt like everything I had ever carried was rising to the surface all at once—my mother, my grandparents, my uncle, my friendships, my childhood.

I had been holding all of it for years. And I was finally reaching the point where I couldn't hold it anymore.

I had carried it all until there was nothing left of me to hold. And that is where the next part of my story begins.

I didn't understand then that grief isn't only about death. Some grief comes from losing people who are still alive. Some grief comes from losing the future you kept hoping for. Some grief comes from realizing that what you waited for isn't coming—and never was.

I thought grief had rules. A beginning. An ending. A funeral. I didn't know grief could be quiet, lingering, confusing. I didn't know it could live in the body long before the mind had words for it.

Rodney's death wasn't just sad—it unraveled something in me that I didn't know was already fragile. To be completely honest, I don't think I've ever fully grieved that man. I lost one of the only men in my life who felt steady and kind without conditions, and that loss was brutal. I know now that I didn't grieve Rodney properly at the time. I just kept going, because that's what I had learned to do. Looking back, I can see how much safety I quietly associated with him, how much I felt protected simply by knowing he existed—and how disorienting, even debilitating it was when that safety disappeared.

I still can't believe I had to say goodbye the way I did. I still can't believe I got to be there with him. He was the biggest, baddest angel of them all—a giant teddy bear with the softest heart. Losing Rodney was one of the most painful, brutal, and challenging gifts I've ever been given. And I say gift carefully, because at the time, it felt like devastation.

This was sacred, even in the breaking

Rodney was always there. I never once questioned his love for me. Even when he wasn't physically present, I never doubted it. I felt it. It was real. It was pure.

There's a night that still lives in my body. I was young. Already confused. Already trying to make sense of something I didn't have words for yet. And instead of being protected, I was blamed.

My dad didn't just misunderstand what had happened—he turned it on me. He said I had allowed it. That I had participated. That it was my fault.

I remember the tone more than anything—sharp, certain, final. The kind of voice that doesn't leave room for truth, only shame.

Rodney was furious when he heard. He stood up for me in a way no one else did. He protected me. He knew.

It took me years to even say that out loud. Years to understand how deeply those words lodged themselves in my nervous system—shaping a shame I didn't yet have language for.

He believed me. And later, when I learned the truth about my biological father—when my sense of identity cracked open all over again—that loss took on even more weight. Rodney loved me like his own daughter. I was his niece, his only heir in the ways that mattered, and that bond was real, regardless of blood. Losing him while simultaneously losing the story I thought I knew about my family was more than grief—it was disorientation at the deepest level.

Grief for my grandparents was complicated. It wasn't dramatic—it was heavy in a slow, accumulating way. I remember their deaths. I remember their funerals. But I don't remember giving myself permission to sit with the memories or the feelings. Death brought out the worst in people—fighting, entitlement, old wounds—and I remember feeling repelled by it all. Watching adults unravel around loss taught me early that grief wasn't safe to express. That you keep it contained. Quiet. Managed.

I remember wanting my grandmother's painting—one of the most meaningful pieces of my childhood—and somehow, impossibly, I have one now, hanging in my living room. The safest place I ever felt as a child, captured on canvas, lives in my home. That isn't coincidence. That's God. There's a whole story there, and one day I'll tell it.

Saying goodbye in person is different. I remember holding Rodney's face. I remember holding my grandparents' faces. That kind of goodbye stays with you forever.

But the hardest grief wasn't for the people I buried. It was for the people I never truly had.

I wasn't just grieving them—I was grieving what I spent my life hoping for: a mother who could take accountability, parents who could protect instead of deflect, and a family where truth didn't cost belonging. I was grieving the fantasy that someday things would shift, that love would finally arrive in the form I needed.

Letting go of that hope felt like free fall. It felt like betrayal layered on top of betrayal.

I didn't just lose relationships. I lost innocence. I lost time. I lost the part of me that still believed waiting long enough would make things right. My body grieved before my mind could catch up. It was nervous-system grief—the kind that shakes you awake and leaves you raw.

Grief arrived when I stopped pretending something was still possible. Healing arrived when I allowed myself to feel it. And somewhere in that process, I realized something else, too: I wasn't broken. I was a survivor.

Emotional abuse doesn't announce itself. It doesn't always look loud or violent. Often, it looks like dismissal. Deflection. Silence.

It looks like taking your pain to someone you love and being met with, "Did you do that?" instead of, "That must have hurt."

What harmed me most wasn't a single moment—it was the pattern. The repeated experience of having my reality questioned. Of being told, directly or indirectly, that my hurt was inconvenient, exaggerated, or somehow my fault.

Over time, my nervous system learned a dangerous lesson: truth costs connection.

So, I learned to soften it. Delay it. Carry it alone.

Emotional abuse trains you to doubt yourself. To overexplain. To stay quiet just to keep the peace. And the hardest part is this—you don't realize it's happening while you're inside it. You just feel small. Confused. Wrong.

Healing didn't suddenly make me angrier. It made me clearer. I didn't become less forgiving. I became less willing to abandon myself.

PART FOUR

THE AWAKENING

CHAPTER 14

High Functioning Isn't the Same as Healed

When I first got sober, life felt both incredible and incredibly strange.

From the outside, it looked like I was doing amazing. I had stopped drinking. I had survived something that nearly killed me. People told me how proud they were of me—and I believed them.

But if I'm honest, those early sober years felt flat. Quiet in a way that wasn't peaceful yet. I hadn't healed anything. I had just removed alcohol.

My body wasn't drowning anymore, but my nervous system was still tangled in trauma. I didn't have language for it yet. I just knew something was off.

During my postpartum season, I was functioning but not thriving. At the time, I told myself this is just how marriage is. This is just how life is.

I didn't have anything inside my body to compare it to.

I didn't question it.

I thought this was just what life felt like.

So, I kept going.

I was sober. I was married. I was a mother.

And I was still struggling in ways I didn't yet understand. I was surviving. And survival felt familiar.

My husband drank alcohol, and we fought about it. Not because he was cruel or explosive—but because my body reacted before my mind could catch up.

The smell of alcohol would hit me, and my body would spin. I didn't know it then, but it took me straight back to being a child around an alcoholic parent.

I tried to explain it gently. Carefully. I didn't want to upset him. Every conversation turned into confusion. I felt like I was attacking him. He felt attacked. And I couldn't understand why it kept going wrong.

I didn't know I was time-traveling.

Motherhood changed me in beautiful ways—and exhausting ones. I stopped asking for help. I told myself this was normal. That relationships are hard. That this is what it costs.

I remember thinking, quietly, *Is this how it's supposed to feel?*

I loved being a mother. Maddie was everything I had dreamed of. And yet, emotionally, something felt missing.

My body knew before my mind did.

A normal weekday actually felt good—comfortable, predictable—especially if I was in my routine. If I had checked all the boxes, my body felt calm. That was the problem, though. The calm was conditional. If something didn't go right, I felt it immediately. My nervous system still wasn't healed—it was managed.

At the time, I truly believed I had fixed a lot. And in some ways, I had. Nutrition and gut health changed the trajectory of my life. I don't say that lightly. It was a huge puzzle piece I had never had before—a healthy one. I felt better physically than I ever had. My mind felt clearer. My energy was steady. Emotionally, things felt more regulated than in any season before.

And even now, I know this matters: from the outside, that version of me would still be labeled "healthy." Admired, even. People would point to the routines, the discipline, the results, and say, "See? That's it. That's health."

The only reason I know it wasn't the whole truth is because of the work I've done in the last four or five years. Trauma work. Nervous system work. Faith. Healing that reached my mind, my body, and my soul—not just my habits. God gave me a renewed mind later. I didn't have that yet.

Back then, I did feel better than I ever had—physically and emotionally.

But I was still deeply lonely—especially in my marriage. I carried that quietly. I couldn't explain it. I would try. I would tell my husband I wanted connection, excitement, growth—something shared. Every time, it seemed to land in resistance, defensiveness, or confusion.

"That's not me. Why do you want me to change?"

There was always a reason he couldn't meet me there.

So, while everything looked perfect from the outside, inside our home I felt isolated and sad. I carried that quietly.

And at the same time, things with my mother were getting more confusing. We went through constant ins and outs—moments that didn't feel right but that I didn't yet have language for. Something in me was starting to shift. I didn't understand it yet—but my body was noticing what my mind hadn't caught up to.

I kept going anyway. That was always my solution.

Looking back now, I can see that this season wasn't failure—it was information.

I had removed alcohol. I had built structure, routines that worked. On the surface, I looked steady—disciplined, productive, even admired. But inside, my nervous system was still running on old wiring—just quieter, more contained.

I didn't yet know how to listen to my body beyond managing it. I didn't know how to rest without guilt. I didn't know how to ask for more without feeling like I was asking for too much. I didn't know that safety was something you could feel—not just something you could negotiate around.

So, I normalized loneliness. I normalized tension. I normalized silencing myself. I normalized doing everything alone and calling it strength.

And my body kept adjusting—accommodating—holding more than it should have had to.

At the time, I told myself I was fine. Better than fine, actually. I told myself this was adulthood. Marriage. Motherhood. Life.

What I didn't realize was that my body was already preparing to interrupt that story.

It was paying attention long before I was.

I didn't know it yet, but this was the season when high functioning stopped being enough—and my body began getting ready to speak in a way I wouldn't be able to ignore.

CHAPTER 15

What I Know Now

It took me years to understand what I had lived through.

Not just the events—but what they did to my body, my mind, and the way I moved through the world.

I didn't have language for it then.

But I do now.

CHAPTER 16

When Therapy Turned the Lights On

I didn't go to therapy because I thought something was "wrong" with me. I went because I was tired of feeling confused. Tired of being almost okay but never settled. I had done all the "right" things—I was sober, married, a mother, functioning—and yet my body still felt like it was bracing for impact. Therapy wasn't a breakdown moment. It was a quiet one. A moment when the lights didn't come on all at once, but they flickered just enough for me to realize I had been living in the dark without knowing it.

I didn't have some dramatic breaking point or blow-up that sent me searching. I didn't even know what I was looking for. But I remember when I finally emailed the therapist I had been recommended—I was terrified. My hands were shaking. I had no idea what to say. I felt exposed before I even walked through the door.

I started therapy in 2020, and I didn't go in saying I wanted a divorce or that my life was falling apart. I went in because I was confused. I was deeply unhappy in my marriage, and I thought therapy would help me understand what I was doing wrong so we could fix it.

I'll never forget something my therapist said to me later. She reminded me that, when she first asked why I thought I needed therapy, I said, "Because of my marriage."

She'd smiled gently and said, "Okay… let's back up for a bit and talk about you. We'll get to that."

Holy moly, was she right.

We had to back up—way back—and heal a lot of Tammy's childhood first.

The first few sessions were uncomfortable. *Really* uncomfortable. I didn't know what to expect. I think I assumed therapy would be advice, tools, and maybe instructions on how to be better. What I didn't expect was feelings. Once we started talking about feelings, something in me cracked open—in the best way. It was like I had been deprived my entire life of emotional language and permission.

I had no idea you were allowed to talk about feelings.

I had no idea you could heal from childhood.

I had no idea silence wasn't required for survival.

I was scared, though. Deeply scared. I felt like I was betraying my husband. Betraying myself. For months, I didn't even tell him I was going to therapy, because I was afraid of what he'd think or say. Looking back, that breaks my heart—and also makes me angry. Therapy wasn't bad. It was healthy. It was meant to help us.

But when I finally told him, he didn't respond well. He didn't want me to go. That part shook me, because deep down I knew I needed it—even though it scared me, too.

I didn't understand it then, but my body felt the resistance immediately.

One of the strangest parts of therapy was realizing how long I had been living in the dark without knowing it. Another strange—and powerful—moment came when my therapist handed me a piece of paper one day and asked me to read it. It was a list of narcissistic traits. I remember that moment like it was yesterday.

As I read through the list, my chest started to feel heavy. When I finished, I handed it back to her and said, "That all feels… extremely familiar."

Every single line checked a box. Not just in my marriage—but in patterns I had lived inside for years, long before I had language for them.

That was one of the first times language landed in my body and didn't bounce off. When I first heard those words—narcissistic, gaslighting, enmeshment—my body went still.

Therapy began revealing something I had never been allowed to consider: I wasn't wrong. I wasn't crazy. I had normalized being minimized because it was all I had ever known.

Slowly, therapy chipped away at the hard wall I'd built around my pain. Not by force—but by witnessing. By listening. By letting me talk. For the first time in my life, I wasn't explaining myself. I was being understood.

A lot came up. Numbness. Abandonment. Rejection. Grief. Anger. Pain. I didn't resist therapy—I clung to it. I went twice a week at first, then weekly for a long time. It became my haven. A place where someone cared enough to listen, validate, and help me make sense of my story.

Therapy didn't give me answers overnight.

It gave me language.
And safety.
And permission to be seen.
That changed everything.

The lights didn't blind me.
They showed me where I'd been living.

CHAPTER 17

Awareness Became a Liability

I didn't know it yet, but my body had already started telling the truth. I just didn't have the language—or the safety—to listen.

On paper, my life looked fine. I was sober. Married. A mother. I was functioning. Showing up. Doing life.

But inside, I felt restless and exhausted in a way I couldn't explain. I kept telling myself this was normal. That this is just what life feels like. My body disagreed.

I normalized patterns in my marriage that I didn't yet have language for. At the time I told myself everything was fine that this was just part of our rhythm. I compared it to where I had come from and convinced myself it was better, and that mattered more than how it felt in my body.

But something in me didn't fully settle into that. My body held a quiet tension I couldn't explain.

I normalized things I didn't yet have language for.

I told myself it was fine. That it was normal. That this is just what life feels like sometimes. On the surface, everything looked steady. I was functioning. Showing up. Doing life.

But inside, something in me felt unsettled in a way I couldn't explain. My body knew before I did.

There were moments that seemed small on the outside but didn't feel that way to me. Subtle shifts in energy. Changes in tone. Things I couldn't fully explain but felt in my body.

My husband and I didn't always see those moments the same way. I tried to explain what I was feeling, but I didn't have the language for it yet—and he didn't always understand it the way I needed him to.

I told myself everything was fine. That this was just part of life, part of being in a relationship. That it was good enough. And for a long time, I believed that. Something in me didn't fully settle into that. My body held a quiet tension I couldn't explain.

Looking back now, I can see it more clearly. It wasn't about blame. It wasn't about labeling anything as good or bad. It was about the moment my awareness began to wake up before I was ready to listen to it.

At the same time, my relationship with my mother felt increasingly confusing. I had been enmeshed with her my entire life. She was all I knew. We were so deeply codependent, I didn't even realize it was abnormal. She was my world—and I was hers—in a way that felt warped and heavy and impossible to explain.

She often couldn't hold eye contact with me for very long. I remember noticing it, even if I didn't fully understand it at the time. When she came over, she would Sometimes bypass my daughter entirely and shift her attention to my husband or whoever else was there it always felt off In a way I couldn't explain–yet but I felt it.

When my husband and I tried to talk, It often didn't land the way I hoped it would. Conversations would shift quickly into explanations, logic, or trying to make sense of things, and I often walked away feeling unsure of myself. I can see now that I struggled with communication, too. I didn't always know how to express what I was feeling in a clear or grounded way. That's part of what drew me to therapy–it was helping me learn how to communicate better not just in my marriage but as a person, a friend, and a mother.

I carried a lot of guilt for wanting more. I questioned myself often—wondering if my needs were too much or hard to understand. I could feel moments where I felt alive and connected to myself but I didn't always feel that reflected back in the ways I needed.

There's something else I remember now—something small but incredibly telling.

My mom would come over and immediately put her phone on speaker. I know that might seem normal to some people, but for me, it always felt different. There was something about it that felt intrusive. It disrupted something in my nervous system every single time and I couldn't really explain why.

One day, she came over unexpectedly. My husband came into the bedroom and said, "Hey, your mom just showed up." I wasn't even dressed yet. She was already inside, loud, her presence immediately felt. Something about that day cracked something open in me.

Later, in the bedroom, I started crying. And for reasons I still don't fully understand, I told my husband—for the first time—that I had been sexually abused as a child.

It wasn't planned. It just came out.

He hugged me. He said he was sorry. He said he didn't know. That was enough for me at the time. What else do you even say in moments like that? It was tender—but also strained. We didn't go deeper. We never did.

What's wild is that my mother was the trigger for that truth to surface. Being around her stirred something so deep, my body finally spoke before my mind could stop it. I remember one day she came over, and there were moments —sharp ones that built on each other. At one point she made a sarcastic comment about my therapist, "Oh I bet you and your therapist have a heyday talking about me huh." Another time, she demanded to see my therapist herself, and when I said no that wasn't an option, she exploded. I found myself doing what I had always done trying to manage her reactions. Learning how to walk around her moods. How to diffuse things the best I could. How to lower my head and move my body just enough to keep the peace.

But something in me was different that day.

As the moments stacked, I could feel it building inside me not loud or dramatic, but undeniable. My body felt unsettled like it was reacting to more than just the moment in front of me. I could feel myself shrinking, my heart racing, trying to manage her instead of honoring myself.

And for the first time, I listened.

She stood in my entryway, towering over me, and said, "Oh, you want me to leave *your* house?" Emphasizing *your* like it wasn't mine. Like I didn't belong there.

When she left, she told me the only thing she wanted from me was access to my daughter.

I was stunned. Hurt. Crushed. Abandoned. Rejected. I couldn't believe it was happening.

And even then, a part of me almost tried to minimize it. Almost tried to keep going like I always had. But something in me knew this moment mattered. My body had finally told the truth and I could not unknow it.

Looking back, I can see that my entire life was filled with these moments. Moments when my body knew something was wrong long before my mind could name it. Moments when I learned to normalize discomfort because questioning it felt more dangerous than enduring it.

And when I finally started therapy, something inside me clicked.

Not all at once. Not dramatically.

But enough to know that the confusion I had lived with my entire life wasn't because I was broken.

It was because I had been surviving.

Healing didn't arrive the way I thought it would. I used to imagine it as relief—like something lifting, easing, and resolving. I thought healing would mean the pain stopped, the anxiety softened, and the noise quieted. I thought I would finally feel better.

What actually happened, though, was different.

Healing turned on the light. And once the light was on, I couldn't turn it back off.

At first, I didn't understand what was happening. I just knew everything felt sharper, louder, and more vivid. I started noticing things I hadn't noticed before: the way people spoke to each other, the way children reached for connection and didn't always receive it, and the way my own body reacted before my mind could explain why.

I remember sitting in a therapy session after a trip, trying to explain how unsettled I felt. I told my therapist I felt overstimulated, almost raw. I described being on an airplane and overhearing a mother repeatedly hushing her child—not harshly, not cruelly, just dismissively. I watched the child look up at her, searching for something and not finding it. I couldn't shake the feeling it left in my body. It stayed with me long after the plane landed.

I remember thinking something was wrong with me.

My therapist looked at me gently and said, "Nothing is wrong. You've just turned on the light."

That sentence changed everything.

Because, once the light is on, you don't just see yourself more clearly—you see everything more clearly. The good. The harmful. The subtle. The familiar patterns you once excused. The ones you survived by. Awareness doesn't make you softer. It makes you truer. And truth has weight.

Healing didn't remove pain from my life. It removed my ability to dissociate from it. It took away the numbness I had mistaken for peace and invited me to stay present in moments that used to send me straight into performance, avoidance, or self-abandonment. It asked me to feel—fully.

That was terrifying.

Because feeling meant I could no longer override myself. I couldn't explain things away. I couldn't pretend certain dynamics were fine when my body knew they weren't. I couldn't keep telling myself that endurance was the same thing as love.

For a long time, survival had been my skill set. I was excellent at it. I could endure discomfort, confusion, emotional inconsistency, and unspoken expectations without ever naming them. I had learned early on how to stay alert, how to read the room, and how to adjust myself to keep things calm.

Healing didn't shame that part of me. It honored her—and then gently asked her to rest.

Because awareness changes the rules. Once you see clearly, you are no longer responsible for maintaining what harms you. You are responsible for choosing differently.

That's when things became complicated.

CHAPTER 18

The Truth About My Father

I will never forget that day.

The truth destabilized me completely. It discombobulated everything I thought I knew about my life, my identity, and my history. And at the same time, it gave me something unexpectedly solid to stand on.

God gave me the truth that no one else was willing to share with me.

Not once.

Not after years.

Not after countless opportunities.

No one—except Him.

Everyone else was wrapped in shame.

February 16, 2023

I remember the date clearly. I won't allow myself to forget it.

I remember the room. I remember the chair being pulled closer to me. I remember the person sitting across from me, visibly emotional, struggling to find the words. In that moment, they felt less like a person and more like a vessel—someone carrying something they didn't know how to hold.

They said, "I don't know how to say this. And I don't know if I'm supposed to. But I feel like I am. I'm going to share with you what I know, and I pray this is the right thing to do."

And then the words came.

"I have reason to believe that Tomp [my stepfather] is your biological father—not Ray who you know as your dad."

I froze.

My body went still. My mind went quiet and loud at the same time. I felt shocked, disoriented, and strangely familiar with the information all at once—as if I had just been told something my soul already recognized, even though I had never had language for it before.

I'm not saying I knew.

I'm saying, in that moment—when being given new information about who I was—it shook everything inside of me and, at the same time, gave me a strange clarity I couldn't yet understand.

I remember calling my husband and asking him to come be with me. I knew, instantly, that whatever happened next, my life had just changed. I didn't know how. I didn't know what I would do. I didn't know what the truth would fully become.

But I knew nothing would be the same.

That day passed in a fog. I was in shock for hours. Coming home felt surreal. Trying to figure out what to say, what to do, or how to feel—it all felt impossible. My nervous system was overwhelmed. Everything inside of me felt scrambled and unsteady.

I kept asking myself, *What do I do next?*

I realized I needed facts. Something tangible. Something concrete to keep my mind from completely spinning out of control. My first thought was to call my doctor.

And then it hit me—I already had an appointment scheduled. Days later. Which was unusual for me.

An appointment with the doctor who had cared for both me and my mother for many years. Not briefly. For most of my life. She was our shared doctor.

That week, I walked into the appointment knowing I was going to ask her face to face if she knew anything.

My heart was racing. My anxiety was through the roof. My blood pressure was so high, she commented on it with concern. I remember internally laughing to myself, thinking, *You have no idea what I'm holding right now.*

When the moment came, I asked her directly. As calmly as I could.

"I would like help," I said. "I'd like to know what you know about Tomp being my biological father."

That's exactly what I said.

I don't know if I can ever fully put her facial expression and body language into words—but it told me everything I needed to know.

She looked at me and asked, "Have you talked to your mother?"

I was stunned by the question.

Have I talked to my mother?

About this?

No. I'm here talking to you.

Moments later, she stood up and said she needed to step outside and make a call. She explained she needed to contact her lawyer to make sure she stayed in compliance with HIPAA laws.

I sat there in shock, not fully understanding what was happening. I told myself, *Okay. Whatever you need to do.*

When she came back into the room, she apologized and said she needed to be careful with what she shared. She told me, again, that she thought I needed to talk to my mother.

I smiled. I laughed. It was pure defense.

Inside my body, everything was screaming: *There is no way!*

There was no world in which I could ask my mother a question like that and expect honesty. We had never been able to talk safely. Why would this be different?

I left that appointment knowing what I needed to know—but still needing proof. Something concrete. Something my brain could anchor to, so I didn't feel completely unmoored.

I still don't fully understand that entire situation. I don't think I ever will.

She had been my doctor for years. She had also been my mother's doctor. And somehow, and all of that, I was the one left without answers.

I understand there were laws. I understand there were boundaries. I understand she was trying to do the right thing by protecting my mother's confidentiality.

But I was her patient too.

And there's still a part of me—if I'm being honest—that doesn't understand how something so foundational to my identity could be withheld from me in the name of protection.

I remember sitting there, feeling like the truth was right in front of me… and still just out of reach. Like everyone else had been entrusted with something about my life that I was the last to know.

And even now, there's a younger part of me that still feels that. Still wonders where my protection was and all of it. Where my advocate was. Where the voice was that said, *she deserves to know.*

I can hold both now—the understanding and the frustration. But that doesn't mean it all makes sense now.

In the first week of March, I sent my mother a letter.

By then, everything between us had already begun to unravel. Communication felt strained, fragile like no matter how carefully I chose my words, we were never quite reaching each other. The volatility, the outbursts, the unpredictability… it had worn something down in me. Talking didn't feel safe. Calling didn't feel safe. Even being around her didn't feel safe anymore.

The emotional weight of that season was overwhelming. I felt it in my chest, in my body, in the way I couldn't think clearly or land anywhere steady.

So I chose what felt safest. What felt most contained.

I wrote a letter.

It was brief. Direct. Clear.

I told her e-mail was the best form of communication. And then I said the thing that changed everything I told her I was aware my father was not my biological father that was all I could hold.

All I knew in that moment was that I was deeply, overwhelmingly sad. This wasn't just information it was a life shift a fork in the road I hadn't chosen but now had to walk.

I knew something in me would have to heal. I knew everything was going to be different.

I just had no idea how.

It felt like I was standing at the beginning of a very long road, with no map no clarity—just the quiet knowing that I had to keep going.

At the time, I thought the hardest part was writing the letter. Saying it out loud. Sending it.

I thought that was the moment everything broke open.

I was wrong.

God didn't ask me to stay where I was breaking.
He led me toward what would heal me.

CHAPTER 19

Boundaries with My Mother

The weeks after I sent that letter to my mother felt like a kind of detox. My nervous system didn't know what to do with the silence. I don't think I did, either.

Everything had shifted so quickly, and yet nothing felt resolved at all. I had said the truth out loud—but I was still living in the aftermath of it.

I remember repeatedly saying to my husband, almost frantically, "I know my mom is going to be freaking out."

I was consumed with her reaction—what she might be thinking, what she might do, how she might respond. It felt like my entire body was bracing for impact.

One time he looked at me and gently said, "Why are you so worried about her response? You don't even know what it will be." Then he paused, really looking at me, and asked something I hadn't let myself fully consider. "Did she ever think about how this would feel for you?" About what it would be like to not know? Did she ever consider what this might do to you…or give you the truth about your own identity?"

He was right. And yet, not caring about my mother felt impossible. My entire nervous system had been wired around her for as long as I could remember.

I checked my phone constantly, like an addict checking for a fix. At the time, I didn't have language for it, but I was deeply entrenched in a trauma bond. I don't think people talk enough about how powerful and destabilizing those bonds are. Breaking them is not just emotional—it's physical. It felt like withdrawal.

That first week of March, I waited for the ball to drop. I knew, once she received the letter, something would come back to me—some reaction, some response. And sure enough, on Thursday, March 9, at noon, I received her email. It came just minutes before I walked into my therapist's office. God's timing felt unmistakable. I needed support for what I was about to read.

Her response was brief and cold. She acknowledged receiving my letter and reiterated that she believed this was not a topic for email, again stating we should discuss it face to face when I was ready. Reading it hit a soft, vulnerable place inside me—one that already knew well about rejection from her. The tone felt familiar. Dismissive. Shaming. Detached.

Even though I had lived with this dynamic for years, something about this moment felt different. My entire identity had been shaken, and in the middle of that devastation, her response felt like confirmation that she was not going to meet me with care. It hurt deeply. It was validation my nervous system didn't want but finally received.

That night, sitting in our living room, I checked my email again. She had sent another message—this time attempting an apology. I remember feeling both terrified and hopeful as I opened it. I wanted so badly to hear from her, and at the same time, I was afraid of her.

The apology wasn't real accountability. It followed the familiar pattern of being "sorry you are hurting," rather than taking responsibility for the harm itself. But even that small shift—her not being openly cruel—felt like relief to my body.

I started crying uncontrollably. I remember laying my head on my husband and sobbing, overwhelmed by how desperate I was for even the smallest amount of decency from my own mother. That realization broke something open in me. I saw, more clearly than ever, how much of my life had been spent managing everyone else's emotions while ignoring my own.

From that point on, I began placing boundaries more intentionally. And I want to be clear about something important: the hardest part of boundaries for me wasn't enforcing them. It was believing I was allowed to have them.

For someone who had endured years of emotional manipulation and enmeshment, choosing distance felt terrifying. Every step away from what hurt me felt like a betrayal of everything I had been conditioned to believe about loyalty and love. But with God's help—and with gentle intention—I kept going.

Months later, just when things had become quiet enough for my nervous system to start exhaling, something happened that shook me all over again.

It was November 2023. I remember my husband walking into the house, looking visibly distraught. I could tell immediately something was wrong.

He asked, "Have you checked your email?"

I said no.

Then, he paused and said, "Your mom sent something."

He didn't explain it right away, but he didn't have to. I could feel instantly that it was serious. My body knew before my mind did.

I remember setting my phone down and pacing the house, trying to prepare myself for whatever I was about to read. At one point, I even walked outside onto the porch, because part of me didn't want to open it. I asked him to just tell me instead.

Maddie was inside. We stood out there together, and I remember the look on his face when he finally said, "Your mother sent a letter from her lawyer."

I just stared at him. "What do you mean?"

And then he told me she was threatening legal action for visitation with Maddie. I genuinely thought he had to be joking.

My mouth dropped open. I remember saying, "Are you serious?" because surely this could not actually be happening.

But it was.

I opened the email and sat there in complete shock. Less than a year earlier, my entire identity had shattered. I had discovered that the man I believed was my biological father was not. I had spent months trying to process the grief, confusion, betrayal, and destabilization that came with that truth. I had tried to communicate honestly. I had asked for accountability, empathy, understanding—something safe to hold onto. Instead, things had only become more fractured.

And now, not even six months after I had begun placing boundaries around the relationship, I was being threatened legally over access to my daughter. I could not believe it.

Even now, saying it out loud still feels surreal.

What struck me most was the entitlement underneath it all. There seems to be this belief in some families that biological connection automatically grants unlimited access—that being a grandparent or relative means you are owed a relationship with someone's child, regardless of how you treat the parent.

But that isn't love. And it isn't safety. Protecting Maddie had become louder than protecting dysfunctional dynamics.

My nervous system reacted immediately. It felt like someone pressing directly into an already open wound. I remember feeling alarmed deep in my body—shaky, nauseated, and unable to fully process that this was real life.

My husband and I both knew we were not okay with what was happening, so we sought legal counsel and tried to approach the situation carefully and reasonably. The door was never shut completely. In fact, we communicated that we were open to moving forward under certain boundaries and requirements that felt emotionally safe for our family. But those conditions were not accepted.

And eventually, it ended there.

I remember feeling deeply relieved when it was over, but also heartbroken that things had reached that point at all. I still don't know that I will ever fully understand how any of it felt acceptable. I only know something in me changed permanently during that season.

CHAPTER 20

What I Thought I Inherited

For so many years, I thought I had inherited damage. Hurt. Pain. Dysfunction. I believed that was the story written into my bloodline. I didn't understand I had also inherited power. Capability. Strength.

I don't know that I have fully grieved the years I believed I wasn't smart. Not intelligent. Not wise. Not capable. But I know I've begun that grief, and even that beginning feels important.

What I didn't see for decades was that the very power inside of me—the intelligence that survived chaos—was the same power that later allowed me to make courageous, life-altering decisions. I never realized I'd inherited that, too.

When you intertwine healing with the cards you were dealt, something extraordinary can happen. There is a blessing in integration. When I began to understand that what I had lived through in nearly fifty years of life was not random but deeply formative—that it could be examined, dissected, and finally understood with love instead of shame—something shifted in me.

That knowledge gave me power. That understanding gave me capability.

It allowed me to trust my instincts. And through that trust, I began to recognize God's whispers—the ones that had been there all along.

The strength I inherited from the man who raised me—my stepfather, who I now understand is my biological father, combined with God and the work of my healing, gave me the internal knowing to make decisions that would have shattered the old version of me. Not just stretched her. Not just scared her. Completely dismantled her.

About eight months ago, before that I began writing this book, I began placing new puzzle pieces into my life. Slowly. Gently. With intention. That strength and healing combination made it clear that our home had to change. It allowed me to move toward an option I had never before been able to entertain. For years, the idea of the ending of my marriage wasn't even something my nervous system could hold. I couldn't look at it. I couldn't imagine it.

But integration changes what you can see.

And once you see clearly, you can't unsee.

It was one massive decision. Then another. Then another. Each one building upon the last. Each one requiring courage I didn't know I possessed. Each one asking me to trust something deeper than fear.

That same inheritance of strength, combined with healing, recently led me to another decision—one that may look different on the surface but required the same internal alignment.

I said yes to a mentor.

I had seen her a year earlier and felt drawn to her spirit, her presence, and her energy. Life moved on, and then she appeared again. I attended a master class. I participated in breathwork—something completely outside my norm. I scheduled a discovery call.

And in that conversation, I felt seen. Held. Safe.

There was something about the container she created—beauty, softness, woundedness meeting strength—that resonated deeply. Saying yes to her mentorship was a big investment. A massive decision. It felt uncomfortable. It felt scary.

And I still said yes. Not just to her. To myself.

I was saying yes to what I knew my nervous system needed. Yes to integration. Yes to breaking patterns. Yes to vulnerability. Yes to choosing what felt both terrifying and aligned. Yes to my heart. Yes to my mind. Yes to my soul.

I was saying yes to the version of Tammy who deserves expansion.

I don't know what the next year will bring. I truly don't. But I'm no longer operating from fear of the unknown. I have developed a deep knowing and trust. I don't have to see every detail ahead of me. I can feel the trajectory.

I can envision beautiful experiences for my daughter and me. I can also anticipate hard ones, because life does not unfold without them. But I no longer doubt my capacity to navigate what comes.

Andrea—this angel—has already impacted me in ways I don't fully have words for yet. I chose to work with her during the publishing process of this book because I knew I needed something I had never truly had before: safety. A steady presence. Someone who could hold space for me as I stepped fully into my voice.

I didn't choose her lightly. It was a leap—one that required trust, both in her and in myself. And even in the short time we've worked together, I can feel something shifting. Not in a loud, dramatic way—but in the quiet, grounded way that tells me something real is happening.

There are people God places in your life who meet you in exactly the season you need them. And then, there are the ones who you know—without needing proof—are meant to stay.

I don't fully understand that yet. But I recognized it.

Keep trusting what I've placed inside of you.
Your body knows. Your spirit recognizes what is safe.
I will continue to place the right people in your path—
right on time.

CHAPTER 21

Grief of Betrayal

What I lost when the betrayal happened was not small. Learning the truth about my biological father was not just a revelation — it was a rupture that opened every older wound still living underneath it.

It wasn't something I could just "let go of" or forgive my way past.

I had to grieve the idea that I had a caring mother—not a perfect one, not a healed one, but one who could see my pain and respond with empathy. I had to grieve the hope that, one day, if I explained it clearly enough or lovingly enough, she would finally say, "I see you. That hurt you. I'm sorry."

I wasn't just grieving her.

I was grieving what I had wanted my entire life.

That loss nearly broke me.

Because the hardest part of betrayal was never what was done to me.

It was what happened after.

Betrayal trauma isn't rooted in the initial harm. It's rooted in the response to it. Or, more accurately, the lack of one. The refusal to take accountability. The inability—or unwillingness—to hold a mirror and say, "That wasn't okay. I hurt you. I'm sorry."

Not a deflection. Not a justification. Not a performative apology meant to keep the peace. But real ownership. Real empathy. Real change.

When that doesn't happen, there is nowhere for healing to land.

People ask why don't I "just forgive." They don't understand that forgiveness isn't the obstacle. *Accountability* is. You cannot move forward in a relationship where the other person refuses to look at themselves. You just end up running on a hamster wheel, replaying the same pain, over and over, hoping this time it will land differently.

It won't.

What made the betrayal unbearable was the constant implication that it was somehow my fault. That my pain was an inconvenience. That my reaction was the problem—not the wound itself. That kind of emotional jabbing doesn't just hurt once. It keeps reopening the injury.

And that's when something in me finally rose up—not cruelty, not bitterness, but clarity.

I wasn't asking for perfection.

I was asking for responsibility.

And when I realized that would never come, I had no choice but to grieve what never truly existed.

That was the real loss

It took me a very long time to find words for this season. Not wisdom—just words. There were days, months, even years when I was grieving something so delicate and painful that language felt impossible. I didn't know how to explain what was happening inside my body or why the ache wouldn't move.

I didn't understand then what I know now: grief makes room. When you allow grief to move through your body instead of trapping it inside, it creates space—space for healing, space for truth, and space for God to place what never could have existed alongside denial. Grief isn't only about death. Some of the deepest grief comes from losing things that were never actually yours to lose.

No one tells you that you can grieve a relationship that still exists—at least in physical form. That was the hardest grief I have ever known. I wasn't just grieving my mother. I was grieving the idea that someday she would become who I needed. I was grieving the human I never really had. I was grieving the dream that she would one day be unconditionally available, that we would learn how to communicate in healthy ways, that love would finally feel safe. I was grieving what I'd waited for my entire life.

The years I lost, not knowing who my father really was.

I was grieving what I didn't get to have—and what would never be possible.

I was grieving the truth I wasn't told about my identity, the years I lost not knowing who my father really was, and the grief of standing at his deathbed without knowing he was my biological father. I was grieving what I didn't get to have—and what would never be possible.

The betrayal didn't just cost me the relationship. It cost me my innocence. It cost me time. It cost me years of understanding myself. I lost my ability to give the benefit of the doubt. I lost the version of myself who still hoped we could have a beautifully, healthy relationship someday.

What I didn't realize then was that my body was grieving long before my mind could catch up. This wasn't just emotional grief—it was nervous system grief. My system had been orienting toward something for decades, desperately anticipating a safety that was never coming. Letting go felt like free fall.

The hardest tears I've ever cried came when I stopped pretending everything was okay. Grief arrived when I allowed myself to be honest—not just in my thoughts, but in my body. When I stopped minimizing. When I stopped explaining. When I stopped hoping. And somewhere inside that grief, something shifted. I realized I wasn't weak for hurting this much. I was a survivor. I had survived decades of emotional deprivation, of waiting, of adapting, of making myself small in order to stay connected. Grief didn't break me—it revealed what I had already endured.

Healing didn't come when I tried to move on. It came when I allowed myself to feel what I had lost. And only then did space begin to open—space for truth, for safety, for new kinds of love to enter.

The Messy Middle

There is a season no one prepares you for—the space after you know something has to change, but before your life actually reflects that knowing. It's not the breaking point, and it's not the freedom on the other side. It's the middle. The part where everything feels undone, but nothing is fully rebuilt yet.

That was where I found myself.

From the outside, it might have looked like I was holding it together. I was still showing up. Still parenting. Still doing the next right thing. But inside, I was carrying a weight I didn't yet have language for. Grief was moving through my body in waves—not dramatic, not constant, but deep and persistent.

I didn't know then that grief doesn't always come from death. Sometimes, it comes from letting go of the life you thought you were building. Sometimes, it comes from releasing the version of yourself who kept surviving because she didn't know another way.

I was learning—slowly and painfully—that clarity doesn't bring immediate peace. It brings responsibility. Once you see the truth, you can't unsee it. And that meant I had to live inside decisions that felt both right and excruciating at the same time.

Some days, I felt strong. Other days, I felt hollow. I questioned myself constantly. Was I doing the right thing? Was I overreacting? Was I strong enough to carry what came next? I wasn't spiraling the way I used to, but I also wasn't calm. My nervous system was adjusting—letting go of familiar chaos while not yet trusting quiet.

What grounded me most during that time was my daughter.

I became acutely aware that she was watching not just what I said, but how I moved through uncertainty. I wasn't trying to be perfect. I was trying to be honest—regulated enough to respond instead of react, steady enough to let her feel safe even when I felt unsure. That mattered more to me than getting anything else "right."

I didn't rush myself through that season. For the first time in my life, I allowed things to be unfinished. I let myself grieve without forcing resolution. I let myself feel proud for simply staying present. And slowly, something shifted. I wasn't trying to escape discomfort anymore. I was learning how to stay with it.

The messy middle taught me that healing doesn't always look like relief. Sometimes, it looks like restraint. Sometimes, it looks like choosing not to abandon yourself just because the outcome isn't clear yet. It looks like breathing through another day without numbing, fixing, or performing.

That season didn't give me answers—but it gave me something better.

It gave me capacity.

And that changed everything.

Some of the most important relationships in my life didn't come from blood. They came from shared survival, laughter in the middle of exhaustion, and God quietly weaving threads I didn't yet recognize.

Marie is one of those threads.

We met more than a decade ago in her salon, where I used to go for pedicures. She's Filipino, vibrant, bold, and beautiful like a firework—the kind of woman who fills a room without trying. What started as a simple service appointment slowly turned into something much deeper.

Over time, she became my client, and I found myself supporting her in business, offering guidance where I could. But what neither of us realized then was that we were becoming sisters.

We've walked through hell together over the last ten years—real life, real loss, and real rebuilding. We've laughed hard, cried harder, and held each other steady through seasons neither of us would have chosen but both of us survived.

She's my Asian bestie turned sister. I'm blonde, she's dark-haired, and somehow, we've always fit. Two peas in a pod, moving through life side by side.

Marie is a God-thread in my story. A reminder that healing doesn't happen in isolation, and that sometimes, the family who saves you doesn't share your last name. But they do share your heart.

Sometimes, the family who saves you
doesn't share your last name…
but they do share your heart.

PART FIVE

THE PEACE PROCESS

CHAPTER 22

Baptism 'cause It Was a Sign

Baptism—April 16, 2023

By April, something in me was ready.

Not because anyone told me I should be.

Not because it was the next "right" spiritual step.

But because my body knew it was time.

What stayed with me most about that day wasn't the water or the crowd or the photos—it was the number. *Sixteen.* April 16. A date that had already imprinted itself into my body long before I understood why.

God had given me the truth about my father on the sixteenth—a truth that changed everything.

So, when I realized my baptism would fall on the same date, it felt impossible to ignore. Not dramatic. Not performative. Just aligned. Familiar. Marked.

This wasn't about religion for me.

It was about choice.

Surrender.

Relationship.

In 2022, Maddie and I had started going to church gently. It wasn't forced, and it didn't feel heavy. It felt soft. Safe. New in a way that made me proud of myself. One of my mother's close friends had encouraged us to come, and because I trusted her, I did.

We began building a quiet rhythm there. We would see familiar faces, sit near people we knew, and slowly let it become something that felt familiar instead of intimidating. I didn't have language for it then, but something in me was opening. Something was softening. God was already doing work in me long before I ever stepped into the water.

And then, February 16, 2023 happened. The day I learned the truth about my father. The day my identity split open.

From that moment on, something in me shifted quickly. I started healing. I started protecting myself. I started setting boundaries. I started talking to God differently—not out of habit, but out of need. Out of surrender.

So, when I later saw there would be a baptism on April 16, I didn't experience it as coincidence.

I knew.

February 16 had been the day God gave me truth. April 16 became the day I gave Him my yes.

It was about saying yes to a faith that had been growing quietly alongside my healing—a faith that didn't demand perfection or performance, but one that met me exactly where I was.

On baptism day, I was told I could choose whomever I wanted to be with me—even in the water. And the moment I heard that, I knew. I chose my therapist. My friend. The woman who had walked with me through some of the most disorienting seasons of my life. The one who taught me how to understand my nervous system. How to feel safe inside my own body. How to stay.

When she said yes, I didn't fully grasp what it would mean until I was standing there. She was the one who gently lowered me into the water. The one who helped bring me back up. Renewed. Grounded. Seen. That moment will stay with me forever. Having her there felt sacred—not because she saved me, but because she had helped me learn how to save myself.

When I went into that water, I wasn't trying to perform anything. I was surrendering.

I was releasing shame. Secrecy. The version of me that had survived by hiding.

I was asking God to meet me in the truth of who I was becoming. To rewire what had been shaped by trauma. To fill the places that had only ever known confusion with something steady. Something true.

I wanted His light in every place I had lived in fear. And because God has a sense of humor, here's what happened next.

My husband and daughter were waiting for me while I went to the bathroom to change. I was gone maybe five minutes. When I came back, my husband said, "Your mom was just here."

I said, "What do you mean, *here*?"

She had come to the stable and talked with them while I was gone.

Of course she did.

I remember laughing—not because it was funny, but because it was so... God. Of course He sent me to the bathroom. Of course the timing worked out that way. I didn't feel shaken or rattled. Just aware. Almost protected. Like a quiet reminder that I didn't have to manage everything anymore.

That day mattered to me. I was proud of myself for taking that step—for choosing surrender, for letting my faith be seen. It felt aligned. It felt right.

What I didn't understand yet was that another loss was unfolding alongside that sacred season.

One of my mother's close friends—someone I had known for years, someone I trusted and looked up to—learned the truth about my father.

And without ever speaking to me, she and her husband quietly stepped away from our lives. It wasn't just distance. It was absence. They had been part of what brought us there, and then suddenly, they were gone.

I remember sitting in those pews with Maddie, looking around, trying to understand what had shifted. I wasn't questioning what I had done—I knew I hadn't done anything wrong. But I could feel the weight of something I didn't fully understand yet.

What I see now is that sometimes people don't know what to do with truth—especially when it brings up something unresolved in them. And instead of moving toward it they move away.

At the time, all I felt was the loss. The confusion. The quiet way it impacted my daughter, too, even if no one meant for it to.

It stayed with me not as blame, but as a reminder: you don't always know how your silence or distance might land in someone else's life. Especially a child's.

It was one of the first times I realized that someone else's discomfort with truth can quietly turn into distance.

I don't live from a victim identity, but I also won't pretend that loss was neutral. My daughter and I felt the impact of someone else's inability to sit with truth.

By the time April 16 came, baptism wasn't just spiritual—it was personal. It was a response to truth. To loss. To God meeting me in the middle of both.

That realization became part of my baptism, too.

Baptism didn't make my life easier. It made me steadier.

It helped me understand that not everyone can walk with me—and this wasn't failure or lack of faith. It was discernment. It showed me how much I had relied on other people to ground me—and how painful it was when they fell away.

God didn't remove the losses.

He steadied me through them.

He kept reminding me that I was safe, even as things continued to fall apart around me. My faith became deeply personal during that time. Not loud. Not performative. Just real. I stopped outsourcing my knowing. I learned how to listen differently. How to stay grounded when the ground shifted.

Looking back now, I can see the thread.

From the truth revealed on February 16 to the baptism on April 16 to the grief that followed—God was already there. Preparing me. Strengthening me. Teaching me how to stand.

Faith didn't save me from the storm.

It gave me a place to stand inside it.

And April 16 will always remind me of that.

Sixteen.
I gave you this number long before you understood why.
Not as pressure. Not as shame. Only as love.
As light. As a quiet knowing
that you were never alone in any of it.

CHAPTER 23

Austin, Structure, and ULTRA

When your identity completely collapses, you don't just grieve—you search for something to stand on.

Two months after my world fell apart, I got on a plane to Austin. Even writing that now, I still pause, because I don't fully understand how I did it.

Just weeks before, I had found out that the man I believed was my father... wasn't. That truth didn't just hurt—it unraveled everything. My sense of identity, my past, my understanding of my own story—it all cracked open at once. And yet, somehow, I evaluated what I needed. I sat with it, examined it, and made a decision that surprised even me: I'm going.

Not with anyone. Not because it felt easy. But because something in me knew I needed to be in that room.

So, I booked the ticket, reserved the hotel room, and for the first time in my life, I chose to go somewhere completely on my own. That alone was new. I had always done things with other people—friends, partners, someone beside me—but this time, it was just me. The only thing that softened the edge of it was knowing a couple of familiar faces would be there. Knowing a couple of familiar faces would be there, women I genuinely loved and respected.

Just knowing I might see them gave my nervous system a small sense of relief. But this trip wasn't about comfort. It was about something deeper.

Before Austin, I had already gone through Brendon Burchard's High Performance Habits course and mentorship. That decision had impacted me in ways I couldn't ignore. The way he spoke about growth, discipline, and intention felt grounded and real—not performative. He made becoming feel possible. So, when I saw he was hosting a live event in Austin, something in me locked in. I didn't know exactly what I would get from it—I just knew I needed to be there.

When I arrived, I remember stepping into the space and feeling something shift almost immediately. Excitement. Pride. A quiet kind of knowing. I couldn't believe I was there—not just physically, but emotionally, mentally, spiritually. I had made a decision in the middle of one of the hardest seasons of my life to show up for myself in a completely different way, and I could feel that.

If you've ever been in a room where Brendon is leading, you know the energy is undeniable. Before he even walks on stage, the music is loud, people are clapping, and there's this build of anticipation.

Then he comes out—dancing, completely himself, a little dorky in the best way—and somehow that makes you feel like you can be, too. He wasn't trying to impress anyone. He was just fully expressed. And that mattered to me more than I expected.

There were so many incredible speakers that weekend, but one that stayed with me deeply was Ed Mylett. He walked out on stage and opened with something I had never heard said so plainly in a room like that: "I am the child of an alcoholic."

I remember sitting there thinking—*Wait... you can say that out loud?* You can be that honest, that vulnerable, in a space like this?

It hit something in me immediately. Here was a man who had built success and influence, and yet he led with truth, not perfection. And I realized that's why he connects with people—because he's not hiding. Sitting there, only two months removed from my own life-altering truth, I felt that in a way I didn't yet have language for.

At one point during the event, we were asked to break into small groups with people we didn't know. I remember feeling my body tense, because I knew what was coming. We were asked to share something we were working through, and I had a choice: stay quiet, keep it surface-level, protect myself—or say it out loud for the first time.

My palms were sweating, my heart was racing, and my voice felt unsteady, but I knew if I didn't start talking about this, I might never be able to.

So, I said it.

I told a group of strangers that just two months earlier, I had found out my entire life had been built on a lie—that the man I thought was my father wasn't. I didn't even know how to explain it fully yet, but I said enough.

And I will never forget what happened next. There was no judgment, no confusion—just presence. Their eyes softened, their energy shifted, and there was this quiet compassion in the room. For the first time, I felt what it was like to speak something out loud and not have it met with silence or avoidance. It wasn't just about being heard. It was about realizing I could talk about it, that I could survive talking about it, that I could begin.

And somewhere in that same weekend, something else happened that stayed with me in a completely different way.

I met Brendon's mom—Mama B.

It wasn't a big, dramatic moment. Just a simple interaction. But I remember exactly how she felt: gentle, kind, safe. There was something about her presence that immediately softened my nervous system. The way she spoke to me, the way she looked at me—it felt grounding in a way I didn't yet understand. Looking back now, I know my body recognized something it hadn't felt in a long time.

By the end of that weekend, I already knew—this wasn't just a good experience. It was a turning point.

So, when Brendon introduced ULTRA, the year-long mentorship, I didn't take it lightly. It was a $10,000 investment, and that number mattered, because I didn't just have that sitting around.

I remember sitting there thinking, how would I even do this? Could I do this? Should I do this? But underneath all of those questions, there was something steadier—a quiet knowing: this is what you need. I had already made the decision before I could fully explain it.

I remember sitting at lunch with my girlfriends afterward—women I admired, successful, confident, established. At the time, I didn't feel like I was on their level. Now, I know that wasn't true, but in that moment, I was still becoming.

They were talking through the decision, weighing it, trying to figure out if they should commit, and I realized something that surprised me—I already had. I had put down the deposit. I was a yes. And for the first time, I wasn't the one looking for direction. I was the one saying, "Do it. Trust yourself."

That moment stayed with me, because it was one of the first times I saw myself differently—not behind, not less than—just someone who chose.

ULTRA didn't fix me. It gave me something to stand on while everything in me was still settling. That year, I showed up month after month—traveling, learning, listening, being uncomfortable, figuring things out on my own. I learned how to navigate airports alone, how to make decisions without asking for permission, how to trust myself in real time. It wasn't dramatic. It was consistent. And slowly, very slowly, something shifted.

I wasn't just healing anymore.

I was rebuilding.

You thought you were starting over.
But you weren't.
You were building—this time on truth.
This time with me.

CHAPTER 24

Mama B & the Plane Ride

God doesn't just remove what hurts us. He replaces it with what heals us.

I think one of the clearest examples of that in my life happened on a plane ride. It was the only time I ever flew into Burbank instead of LAX. I didn't think much of it at the time, but the flight schedule was better, so I decided to try it.

In the Las Vegas airport, I noticed Brendon's mom immediately. She had the brightest red hair. A familiar face. Someone I recognized. Someone I had seen before and knew of through ULTRA and Brendon's work.

My heart totally wanted to walk up and talk to her, but the airport was loud, crowded, and moving fast. Old instincts kicked in. Don't interrupt. Don't impose. Don't assume you belong in the conversation.

So, I waited.

Then, I boarded the plane and realized God had seated me directly next to her. We talked for the entire flight.

Not small talk. Not surface-level pleasantries. Real conversation. The kind that opens without effort. I shared pieces of my story—the grief, the unraveling, the healing, and the sadness I was still learning how to carry. She shared hers—stories of family, of travel, and of a life lived with depth and wisdom.

There was no fixing. No advice. No urgency.

Just presence.

She listened in a way my nervous system recognized immediately—calm, steady, interested, not extracting anything from me. I didn't have to perform. I didn't have to earn her attention. I didn't have to explain myself into being understood.

She saw me.

That day marked the beginning of a relationship that would quietly change my life. I came to know her as Mama B—a name that wasn't assigned but was felt. She became a consistent, grounding presence in my life. Safe. Encouraging. Wise. Not demanding. Not possessive. Not conditional.

She reminded me—without ever saying it directly—that I was worthy of care. That my voice mattered. That I didn't have to shrink to be accepted.

Looking back now, I truly believe God knew exactly what He was doing when He placed us on that plane together. At a time when my nervous system barely trusted people, He gave me a connection that felt safe, calm, and sincere.

There was something so grounding about her. She was thoughtful, steady, genuinely kind, and so easy to talk to. Nothing felt forced around her. I didn't feel like I had to earn her warmth or prove myself worthy of it. She just met me with care.

Sometimes, it's the smallest things that undo me in the best way. The quiet chills that move through my body when

I remember how God set up that meeting. The soft goosebumps that rise when my phone lights up and I see her name. *"Hi, sweetie!"* Or, *"My dearest Tammy."* I still catch myself smiling before I even open the message.

It still feels unreal sometimes—like God, Himself reaches for my phone, just to remind me what safe love sounds like.

The way she speaks to me matters. Not performative. Not excessive. Just steady, warm, and sincere. It settles my nervous system instantly. It's not gold—it's silver. Beautiful because it's trusted. Beautiful because it's real. She isn't trying to fill a hole or fix a wound. She simply shows up as herself—a safe, grounded woman who sees me and believes in me. That kind of love doesn't rush. It doesn't demand. It rests. And every time I feel it, I know—this is God's doing.

CHAPTER 25

Estrangement: When Distance is the Boundary

Before I could walk away, I had to understand why I kept going back. And the truth is, I went back for a long time.

I kept going back because, for most of my life, pain felt familiar. It was what I knew. The back and forth, the tension, the hope that maybe this time it would be different—I was conditioned to live inside that cycle.

Every time we talked, I would try again. I would explain what I needed, hope to be heard, and hope to be met with care. And every time, it would fall apart. But she is my mom. And I wanted—so deeply—to be loved by her. That hope kept pulling me back.

I didn't have language for it then, but I was living inside a pattern that had been formed long before I understood it. I was taught to stay quiet. We didn't talk about feelings. And when I did speak up—whether it was pain, grief, or something that didn't feel right—it was dismissed. Over and over again. Eventually, you stop trusting your own voice.

We were deeply enmeshed for most of my life. I didn't know where I ended and she began. There was a dependence—emotional and at times financial—that made it even harder to step away. And there were always strings attached. I thought that was normal. I thought that was love.

It wasn't I began therapy in 2022 that things started to make sense. I began to understand trauma bonds—the way you can feel tied to someone not because it's healthy, but because it's familiar. Because your nervous system has learned to equate chaos with connection. That awareness didn't come all at once, but when it did, I couldn't unsee it.

What I also had to face was the grief—not of losing a mother, but of grieving one who is still alive. Grieving the relationship I hoped for. The version of her I believed in. The mother-daughter connection I carried in my mind for years but never truly had. That kind of grief is quiet, complicated, and hard to explain. But it was necessary.

And slowly, I began to choose differently.

Estrangement gave me things that my staying attached never could.

It gave me the chance to heal.

I didn't understand that at first. I had to live it to know it was true. There is a saying people repeat casually: you can't heal in the environment that made you sick. But when you are the one living inside that environment, the truth of it is anything but casual. It is embodied. It is unavoidable.

Healing requires space.

Not metaphorical space.

Actual distance.

You cannot feel your way back to yourself while the same toxic patterns are still attached to you, interrupting you, manipulating you, or pulling you back into survival. You cannot create a safe internal mess—the kind where real healing happens—when the source of harm remains active and present in your nervous system.

For me, estrangement was not rejection.

It was protection.

Going no-contact with my mother was one of the hardest decisions of my life. And I need to be very clear about this: people do not cut ties with their parents lightly. Estrangement is not a trend. It is not impulsive. It is not born from anger. It is what happens when every other option has been exhausted.

I tried everything before I chose distance.

Everything.

I spent decades trying to understand her, soften her, please her, accommodate her, protect her, and repair what she refused to acknowledge. I was deeply codependent and completely enmeshed—forty years of my life shaped around keeping the relationship intact, even when it cost me myself.

That matters.

Because the myth surrounding estrangement is cruel. There is a pervasive narrative that adult children who step away from their parents are bitter, ungrateful, dramatic, or disloyal. That narrative is not just wrong—it is harmful. It erases the reality of survivors.

Let me say this plainly: no survivor wants estrangement.

I would have paid money—real money—for the important people in my life to receive the healing they needed. I would have done almost anything. But healing cannot be outsourced. Accountability cannot be forced. And shame will keep people trapped far longer than truth ever could.

What I learned is this: when someone refuses to take responsibility for their harm, the relationship reaches a fork in the road. And I was no longer willing to sacrifice my mental, emotional, and physical safety to protect someone else's denial.

Boundaries with toxic people are not respected. They are challenged, undermined, manipulated, and punished. Anyone who has lived this knows exactly what I mean. When boundaries fail, distance becomes the boundary.

That is not cruelty.

That is clarity.

People often assume my estrangement is about what I later learned regarding my father. I want to be unequivocally clear: that is not why my mother and I became estranged.

The estrangement happened because I asked for honesty, accountability, and safety—and was told, explicitly, that I was still not deserving of the truth.

I was forty-seven years old when my mother told me there had never been a time when she believed I could handle knowing who my father really was. *Forty-seven.* After forty years of emotional enmeshment, caretaking, loyalty, and silence.

That letter arrived on my daughter's birthday.

That moment clarified everything.

It wasn't just the lie.

It was the continued withholding.

The refusal to see me as a full human being worthy of truth.

I want to be very careful here, but also very honest: I have receipts. Letters. Messages. Conversations. I don't need to share them to validate my reality. My nervous system already did that work for me.

Estrangement was not an act of anger.

It was an act of self-preservation. It was out of desperation to *HEAL*.

I am not bitter. I am not vengeful. I am not trying to punish anyone. Although for the ones who understand, punishment will typically be their "excuse," and the entire blame will be placed on you. It's the disgusting truth of continued narcissistic or emotionally unavailable humans.

I am choosing safety—for my body, for my healing, and for my daughter. I will not continue patterns that require me to disappear in order to maintain connection.

So, when people ask, "How could you do that to your mother?" I ask a different question:

"What happened before it got to that point?"

Because estrangement is never the beginning of the story.

It is the last chapter of one that went unheard for far too long.

Many emotionally immature parents believe their adult children are asking them to be perfect.

That is not what is happening.

This belief is a cognitive distortion—feedback gets exaggerated to an extreme so it can be dismissed entirely. If I am not perfect, then I am a terrible parent. And if I am a terrible parent, I don't have to listen at all.

This kind of black-and-white thinking allows accountability to be avoided by collapsing into shame or defensiveness instead of growth.

Adult children are asking for something far simpler.

Accountability.

Repair.

Emotional presence.

The ability to tolerate discomfort without turning away, shutting down, or making the conversation about yourself.

That's not perfection.

That's maturity.

If there was something I wish others understood more it would be that no survivor wants estrangement. We choose it when there is no other way to be safe.

You literally cannot heal while remaining attached to the harm.

CHAPTER 26

When Distance Creates a Ripple

One thing no one prepares you for when you set a boundary—especially with a parent—is how far the ripple travels. Estrangement is rarely contained to one relationship. It rearranges the room.

When I created distance from my mother so I could heal, it didn't just affect us. It fractured other relationships in her orbit, including her sister and her sister-in-law. Women who were not present for the truth of my life, my body, or my healing suddenly felt entitled to weigh in.

One message, in particular, lodged itself in my body: "I don't think God would be happy with your decision or what you're doing."

That sentence landed in the middle of the most sincere, grounded faith journey of my life—a season when I was listening closely, praying honestly, and following God with more humility than I ever had before. And it devastated me. Not because I doubted God, but because His name was being used to shame me.

This is a specific kind of harm—religious abuse dressed up as concern, emotional manipulation disguised as prayer. It sounds holy, but it isn't kind. And kindness is never optional when faith is involved.

If your instinct is to tell yourself, *She was just worried… She meant well… She wanted to help*—pause. This is where motive matters. The motive wasn't protection. It wasn't curiosity. It wasn't care. The motive was judgment, wrapped in Scripture so it couldn't be questioned.

I remember staring at that message, feeling a familiar wave of shame try to move through my body—the old reflex: You've disappointed someone. You've done something wrong. You should explain yourself.

But something had changed. I didn't explain. I didn't defend. I didn't perform repentance for a boundary that was saving my life. Instead, I let the truth settle: Any belief system that requires you to stay unsafe is not sacred.

People often assume estrangement is fueled by anger. In reality, it's fueled by clarity. And clarity has a cost. You lose people who benefited from your silence. You lose people who preferred the version of you that stayed small. You lose people who confuse obedience with endurance.

I didn't lose family because I stopped loving them. I lost them because I stopped abandoning myself. And I made peace with that.

There were so many years when I looked functional, capable, even successful, while quietly unraveling inside.

I've learned this the hard way: You never know what someone is carrying.

There were seasons when I felt like I was screaming inside a glass bubble—everything loud, everything urgent, and no one could hear me. Not a single person.

That kind of loneliness leaves a mark.

Especially when the loss you're grieving is someone who is still alive.

CHAPTER 27

EMDR: When My Body Finally Caught Up

EMDR changed my life in ways I didn't understand at first—and honestly, in ways I couldn't have talked myself into.

Before EMDR, I had insight. I knew my story. I could explain my patterns. I understood trauma intellectually. I could connect the dots, name the wounds, even speak compassionately about my past. But my body didn't know it was safe. I was still bracing. Still scanning. Still living as if something bad was about to happen.

EMDR was the missing link between knowing and being free.

It didn't erase my memories—it removed their power. It allowed my nervous system to finish what it never got to complete while I was surviving. And once that happened, everything else shifted quietly, steadily, and gently.

I remember when my therapist first mentioned EMDR. I had absolutely no idea what it was. I'd never even heard of it. I remember thinking, *God forbid I'm supposed to remember what that acronym stands for—there's no way I'm going to do well with this.* That still makes me laugh.

She asked me if I'd be willing to try it. I said, "I think so… But what is it?"

She explained that it was a form of therapy that uses bilateral stimulation—things like a light bar or tapping—to help the brain reprocess old memories and wounds that never fully resolved. She told me it could feel strange and uncomfortable at first. I was intrigued enough to say yes.

The first time we did it, it felt weird. Really weird. Uncomfortable. Disorienting. And exactly like she said it would. EMDR is wild like that.

There are a few things I would tell anyone considering it—especially if you're healing from childhood trauma. Everyone heals differently. What works for one person might not work for another. But EMDR didn't just help me—it changed my day-to-day life.

This kind of therapy—sitting with my trauma, letting my body lead instead of my thoughts—opened pathways in my brain that had never been accessible before. It was hard work. I had to sit with things that were deeply uncomfortable. I don't have clear memories of much of my childhood, and EMDR helped put pieces together without forcing me to relive everything in detail.

It wasn't about remembering more. It was about releasing what my body had been holding.

EMDR is deeply somatic. It involves noticing where things live in your body—something I had never understood before. My body remembered things my mind didn't. And honestly, it probably still does. That's okay. Just understanding that truth alone was freeing.

EMDR replaced the looping, intrusive sensations and images my body carried from abuse, neglect, and early harm—things I couldn't consciously recall but absolutely felt. It didn't erase my past. It softened it. It quieted it.

One of the biggest things EMDR taught me is this: surrender matters.

You can't force this work. You have to be willing. You have to trust the process. And you have to trust the human you're doing it with. Safety is everything. When you feel safe, you allow yourself to feel. And when you feel, you heal.

I had to let my body and mind go where they needed to go—without controlling it, without narrating it, without judging it. That alone was healing for someone who had spent her whole life trying to manage everything.

I would come out of sessions completely drained. Empty. Exhausted. Sometimes, I'd cry out of nowhere. Sometimes, I'd yawn uncontrollably—deep, full-body yawns that felt oddly relieving. I later learned that yawning helps reset the nervous system. My body already knew.

EMDR taught me that our bodies remember everything.

EMDR taught me that healing doesn't always come through words.

EMDR taught me that God uses many tools—and this was one of them.

I believe EMDR is a gift. A tool God uses to restore what trauma interrupts. It gave me new pathways—not just in my brain, but in my faith. I could finally hear God's whispers without fear flooding my system. I could believe safety was real. I could rest.

Healing didn't make me perfect. It made me present.

My work isn't done. My healing isn't finished. But EMDR gave me my breath back. And that changed everything.

CHAPTER 28

What Travel Did for Me

Travel is something I never imagined would become such a meaningful part of my life. Truly. I never thought I would be the woman who went places—who stepped into that version of herself and felt at home there. I couldn't have predicted how much I would love it or how deeply it would confirm that my healing was real.

Standing in places that took my breath away—oceans, mountains, or cities I never imagined I'd see—did something quiet and profound inside me. Some of those trips happened before I was fully healed, but even then, they stirred something in me. Beauty has a way of doing that. Nature, fullness, wonder—God uses those, too.

Somewhere along the way—without making a formal decision or even realizing it at first—I began to slowly trust myself.

Not loudly. Not confidently. Not perfectly. B+ut enough to notice the difference.

One of the earliest places this trust began to form was in motherhood.

In early 2021, when Maddie was five or six, I remember having a simple thought: it would be really special to have time alone with her. Just the two of us. No distractions. No managing everyone else's needs. Just mother and daughter, together.

The moment that thought appeared, another one followed immediately: *Who do you think you are?*

It was firm. Sharp. Familiar.

My nervous system shut the idea down almost instantly. The part of me that had learned to doubt myself—to outsource decisions, to seek permission, and to question my own capability—took over. The idea of taking my daughter on a trip by myself felt to my body. It wasn't just fear. It was disbelief. I didn't know yet how disconnected I was from my own sense of agency, but I could feel the resistance clearly.

I remember having to convince myself over and over:

- ✧ I deserve this.
- ✧ I am capable.
- ✧ I am her mother.
- ✧ I can do this.

Even saying those words felt foreign at the time.

I questioned myself constantly while planning that first trip. I checked and rechecked every detail. I second-guessed my decisions. I brought it up to my husband repeatedly, almost looking for reassurance that I was allowed to do this, that I wasn't irresponsible or unrealistic or asking too much of myself.

He didn't seem particularly invested in the idea at first. It didn't register as a big deal to him. But to me, it felt monumental.

I decided on Florida for our very first mother-daughter trip—Clearwater Beach, specifically. Maddie was around six years old, and we stayed at the Sandpearl. I remember feeling both excited and nervous leading up to it, like I was stepping into something I hadn't fully proven to myself I could do yet.

We got there early enough that first day to go straight out to the ocean. The sun was beginning to set, and everything felt soft and golden. I can still see it so clearly—Maddie running toward the water, completely unafraid, carrying the little sand toys we had packed. She dropped down into the sand and started playing like she had been there a hundred times before.

I stood there for a moment, just watching her. The sand in our toes, the sound of the waves, the sky shifting colors—it all felt almost surreal. I remember thinking, I can't believe I did this. Something that had once felt so big, so out of reach, was suddenly right in front of me.

That first night, before the sun fully went down, she looked up at me and said, "Mommy, this is so beautiful. I love it here."

And I felt it in my whole body. Not just joy—but something deeper. A sense of this is what life is supposed to feel like.

Before that trip, my body didn't have the capacity for this kind of expansion. I was still wired for survival. I wouldn't have chosen something like this. It would have felt too much, too uncertain, maybe even irresponsible. My mind would have found a way to talk me out of it.

But something had shifted.

Booking that trip—following through on it—did more than create a memory. It showed me that I was capable. That I was allowed to create a life that felt good. That I could be present, not just responsible. That I could give my daughter experiences rooted in joy, not just structure or survival.

That was the beginning of something for me. It was the moment I started becoming a woman who chooses experiences. A woman who trusts herself. A woman who allows life to be good.

And more than that—it was the beginning of becoming the kind of mother I wanted to be. Not just a fun mom, but a safe one. A present one. A mother who creates meaningful experiences filled with love, nature, and connection.

Looking back now, I can see that it wasn't just a trip.

It was a shift.

What surprised me most was how my body responded.

I noticed something new: before this, I could receive beauty without bracing. Yet now, I wasn't rushing. I wasn't scanning for danger. I wasn't waiting for something to go wrong. I was present. Grateful. Open.

That's what nature and beauty do for me—they remind me that survival is not the same thing as living. That my life is expansive, not small. That I am allowed to take up space in the world.

I wouldn't trade those experiences for anything. And now, looking ahead, what fills my heart most is imagining more of the world through Maddie's eyes. Teaching her—not through words, but through experience—that joy, safety, curiosity, and wonder belong to her, too.

I can already picture it: looking over years from now and seeing her smile, knowing she caught the travel bug. Knowing she understands that it is experiences, connection, faith, and the goodness God places in the world that make life rich and meaningful.

Travel didn't just show me the world.

It showed me who I was becoming.

CHAPTER 29

When I Finally Had Words for It

I'll never forget the day my beautiful cousin asked, gently, "What is CPTSD?"

It was early in my healing journey—the season when I had just begun learning the language of my own survival. I remember feeling deeply grateful that she cared enough to ask and, at the same time, completely stuck. Because, even though I finally had words for what I'd been living with my entire life, I still didn't know how to say them out loud. I understood it in my head, but my heart hadn't caught up yet.

What stayed with me wasn't the question itself. It was how she asked. She didn't assume. She didn't rush me. She didn't change the subject when things felt tender. She leaned in. And that mattered more than she'll ever know.

We never did finish that conversation. It's been a couple of years now. But when I recently scrolled through old messages between us, I found something that healed a place in me I didn't even realize was still bleeding.

She had written, *"I can't believe you're being hurt by family like this."*

Those words landed differently because they came from my blood family. I felt seen. I felt believed. I felt chosen. And in that moment, God reminded me of something I desperately needed to remember: not everyone will harm me. Not everyone will twist my truth or silence my voice. Her love became living proof that goodness still runs through my lineage. That redemption can flow through the same veins that once carried pain.

And the most beautiful part is this: I don't need those old texts anymore to prove her love. I don't need evidence. I feel it now—in my body, in my spirit—because that's where God meets me every single time I ask.

Now, I can talk about CPTSD with a steadiness I didn't have before.

Complex Post-Traumatic Stress Disorder gave me my first full breath after years of holding it in. Hearing there was a name for what I'd lived through felt like finding the missing translation for my own life. It meant I wasn't broken. I was responding exactly the way a nervous system responds when it's shaped by repeated trauma.

I still remember the day I finally asked my therapist, "Do I have CPTSD?"

She looked at me with that familiar calm—steady, compassionate—and said, "Yes, Tammy. We've talked about this."

And in that moment, shame and relief collided. A part of me felt foolish for not realizing it sooner. Another part of me finally felt validated.

She reminded me gently, "Of course you have CPTSD. This is what we've been working through for years—

repeated trauma, emotional neglect, survival patterns that shaped your entire childhood."

That conversation changed everything. I had heard of PTSD before, the kind that comes from a single, life altering moment. An accident. An assault. A sudden loss.

But what I was experiencing was different.

It wasn't one moment. It was many.

It was what happens when your nervous system is shaped over time—by unpredictability, by emotional neglect, abandonment, by never quite feeling safe enough to fully rest. It was growing up learning to stay alert to read the room to anticipate.

Not because I was broken, but because my body had learned how to survive.

PTSD survivors know the impact of one earth-shattering moment.

CPTSD survivors know what it's like to live inside the earthquake.

Both matter. Both are real. Both deserve healing.

There's a part of CPTSD no one prepares you for—how deeply it lives in the body.

I remember standing in my kitchen years ago, holding a box with a brand-new electric toothbrush. Something so small. Something so ordinary. And suddenly, my brain couldn't sequence the steps. I froze. Not because it was hard—but because my nervous system short-circuited. Something in me went limp.

I remember thinking, *Is this what my therapist meant? Is this what CPTSD does?*

I asked my husband for help while minimizing my need, smiling through it. "I know this seems silly… I know I should be able to do this…"

But inside, I knew exactly what was happening—and I didn't yet have the language to explain it.

That's the quiet reality of CPTSD. It doesn't always show up in dramatic ways. Sometimes, it shows up in small, ordinary moments—decision-making, transitions, overwhelm—where your body reacts before your mind can catch up.

Healing taught me to notice those moments without shame.

Recently, I found myself navigating things that once would have shut me down—like replacing a washer, handling unexpected expenses, and making decisions without asking anyone if I was doing it "right." And the win wasn't the task itself. The win was that I stayed regulated. I didn't spiral. I didn't need permission.

That's new.

When the delivery men hauled away my old washer, a familiar scarcity voice rose up—*maybe I can sell it, maybe I'll need it, don't waste it.* That old survival loop. But this time, I noticed it, honored it, and chose differently.

I didn't keep what was taking up space.

These are the moments no one talks about. The small pauses. The quiet rewiring. Healing doesn't just show up in big breakthroughs. It shows up in choosing differently in ordinary moments.

And that's how I know I'm healing—not because everything is easy, but because I'm aware. I pause. I choose. I trust.

I'm not walking fast. I'm walking muddy. Sometimes tired. Sometimes unsure.

But I am walking.

And I'm not walking alone.

Understanding my CPTSD didn't make me fragile—it made me honest.

It helped me see that what I inherited wasn't weakness, but survival. And survival kept me alive until healing could arrive.

But survival was never meant to be the final legacy. Once I could name what my body had been carrying, I could finally choose something different—not just for myself, but for my daughter.

I realized then that healing isn't just personal work. It's generational work. What I was learning how to regulate, release, and repair in my own nervous system wasn't just changing me. It was quietly shaping what would be passed down.

And that's when inheritance began to mean something new.

There's something I didn't understand about trauma until I was on the other side of it. When people think about abuse, they often think about what can be clearly named—the words, the behaviors, the moments that hurt. And yes, those things matter. They leave marks.

But what I wasn't prepared for was the confusion.

Not just, "I don't understand what happened," but a deeper kind of disorientation—a loss of clarity that makes it hard to trust your own perception. When you've lived inside emotionally manipulative or dysregulated environments, especially over time, your inner world fills with questions that don't have clean answers.

Was it intentional?

Did they mean to hurt me?

Am I overreacting?

Should I feel this way?

How can someone who says they love me make me feel like this?

And maybe the hardest question of all: *Can I trust myself?*

That question doesn't just pass through your mind—it settles in your body. Especially when the person who caused the harm is someone who was supposed to love you differently. A parent. A partner. Someone who held a place that was meant to feel safe.

When love and harm exist in the same space, your mind doesn't know where to land. Over time, that confusion doesn't just hurt, it disconnects you from yourself.

Complex PTSD isn't only about what happened to you. It's about what happened inside of you because of it. Your instincts get questioned. Your perceptions feel unreliable. Your sense of truth becomes blurry.

It's not just pain—it's uncertainty. And that uncertainty lingers long after the environment changes.

Healing, I've learned, isn't just about acknowledging what happened. It's about slowly learning how to trust your own reality again. To say, without minimizing or over-explaining: This is what I experienced. And how it impacted me. That truth gets to stand—regardless of someone else's intention.

For a long time, I tried to sort it all out perfectly. I wanted to label everything, to make it make sense. But healing didn't come from having every answer.

It came from allowing myself to stop arguing with my own experience. To stop shrinking it. To sit with what I felt without rushing to justify it.

And slowly, something began to return:

Clarity.

Grounding.

A quiet, steady knowing.

Not loud or forceful. Just rooted.

The kind of knowing that says: "I trust myself again."

If you've lived through emotional manipulation, control, or relational patterns that blurred the line between love and harm, I want you to know this:

What you're feeling is not weakness.

It's not "too much." It's the natural response of a nervous system that adapted to survive confusion.

And if the hardest part hasn't just been the pain but the questioning—the unraveling of your own certainty—you are not alone in that.

There is a way back to yourself. To clarity. To truth. To trust.

And while that path can feel slow, layered, and incredibly tender… it is also sacred.

Because, on the other side of that confusion is a version of you who no longer abandons herself to make sense of someone else.

And *that* is one of the most beautiful things.

A version of you who no longer abandons herself
to make sense of someone else.

The version who can finally hear the whisper that was guiding her all along. The version of you who can finally hear that whisper… is also the version of you who begins to make different choices.

To walk away from someone whom you care about—someone you love—because they are unable to meet you in the ways you need… is one of the most courageous things a person can do.

It doesn't always look brave from the outside. Sometimes it looks like grief, like second-guessing, like sitting alone holding both love and truth in the same breath. But at its core, it is a decision to choose yourself.

And not in a surface-level way. Not in a performative, "self-care" kind of way—but in a soul-level way. The kind that asks you to become honest about what you know deep down, what you've maybe always known, but weren't ready to face.

Because there comes a point in healing where you realize something that is both freeing and heartbreaking: you cannot live the life you feel called to live while staying in spaces that require you to abandon yourself. You can't fully step into your truth while constantly negotiating your worth, and you can't answer what's been placed on your heart while trying to maintain relationships that ask you to stay small, quiet, or unsure.

And that realization changes everything.

Because it's no longer about whether you love them. It's about whether you're willing to leave yourself.

For me, that was the shift.

Choosing to walk away wasn't about rejection or punishment—And it wasn't about placing blame.

It came from a quieter place, one where I could no longer ignore what my soul was asking of me.

A need to live differently. To respond differently. To trust myself enough to follow it.

It was about no longer being able to ignore what my soul was asking of me. To live differently. To choose differently. To trust myself enough to follow it.

And that kind of choice… the kind that requires you to hold grief and truth at the same time… is one of the bravest things we can do.

I don't think I ever fully grieved all the people who meant so much to me—my grandma, my grandpa, even my Uncle Rodney.

Not because I didn't love them, but because life didn't really pause long enough for me to feel it. And even if it had, I don't think I would have known how.

I kept moving.

That's what I knew how to do.

But just because I didn't stop to feel it… doesn't mean my body didn't carry it.

I've been carrying grief longer than I ever realized—and in ways I didn't yet understand.

CHAPTER 30

The Revelation

Days, weeks, hours—even minutes—after I created distance from my mom, it felt almost debilitating to my mind and body.

I remember feeling deep hurt. Grief. A heaviness that settled into me in a way I didn't yet understand. It all felt incredibly hard... and confusing. I didn't have language for it at the time. I just knew something inside me had shifted, and I didn't know how to steady myself.

I remember sitting in therapy, asking, "What do I do? What is happening to me?"

I told her I felt numb... like I couldn't fully access what was going on inside my own body.

She gently explained that I was most likely in shock—that what I was feeling made sense. She told me it might take some time, but she would help me through it. That I wouldn't have to navigate it alone. That she would hold space for me while I figured it out.

And I held onto that.

I started going every week—sometimes twice a week—just to make sure I had somewhere safe to land. Somewhere I could release what I didn't yet understand. Somewhere I could be honest about how much it hurt.

Because the truth was, the days didn't just pass—they *poured*.

Tears would come out of nowhere. Even after I thought I was feeling better. I'd have a few steady days, and then suddenly, I'd be right back in it—overcome with grief, caught off guard by how deep it still went.

I remember standing in the bathroom, crying so hard I had to brace myself against the counter. Not just crying—but grieving. Feeling this ache I couldn't quite name yet, only that it felt like loss.

At the time, I didn't understand what I was grieving.

I thought I was reacting to the moment… to the letter… to the distance.

But my therapist helped me see something deeper.

I wasn't just grieving what had happened—I was grieving what I had always hoped for. The relationship I thought we could have. The version of her I had held onto for so long.

And that realization shifted everything…

Because there was no immediate relief after I sent that letter. Not in those early days. Not even close. If anything, it felt heavier before it felt lighter.

I think I believed that distance would bring peace.

Instead, it brought silence. And I didn't know what to do with that.

The quiet in my body was something else entirely. Not calm—just unfamiliar.

And yet, even in the middle of that, I was proud of myself. Because, for the first time, I was intentional about taking care of myself in it.

I showed up to therapy. I let myself be supported. I gave my body what it needed—massages, rest, space to release. I did everything I could to help myself move through it… not just from that moment, but from everything that had led up to it.

From the last year.

From the last forty.

I didn't understand all of it yet.

But I stayed with myself anyway.

CHAPTER 31

The Cost of Not Being Believed

One of the deepest costs of not being believed was what it did to my body. When my truth had nowhere to land, my nervous system stayed in survival. I learned to function, perform, and keep going, but inside, I was unraveling.

The dysregulation showed up as anxiety, exhaustion, hyper-vigilance—and eventually CPTSD. Not being believed didn't just hurt emotionally. It fractured my sense of safety and trust, and over time, it impacted my health. I carried everything inward, and my body paid the price.

Being believed later—not by everyone, but by God—became a turning point in my healing. I didn't need validation or permission anymore. I needed truth to be witnessed and held. That believing wasn't loud or dramatic; it was steady, embodied, and grounding. It allowed integration instead of explanation. My body could finally exhale.

That shift—from needing proof to trusting what I knew—became one of the most healing experiences of my life.

TODAY IS 111:

A Holy Alignment

I am standing in the doorway between what was and what is becoming.
I feel the fear, the grief, the awe, and the excitement all at once—
and God is here in all of it.
Even the money, even the loss, even the injustice—
He is making streams in this desert.
I release what I cannot control.
I keep what is sacred.
And I walk forward as the author of my own story.

There was one Thanksgiving I didn't spend around a table. There was no crowd, no noise to hide behind, and no pretending my way through the day.

It was the longest I had ever been away from my daughter—four nights that stretched my nervous system in ways I didn't know were possible. I didn't choose it because it felt right. I chose it because it was required.

That week asked everything of me.

There were moments I thought I might break—moments when the ache of separation hit so hard, it stole my breath. And still, I kept going. I made plans so I wouldn't collapse. I reached out instead of retreating. God sent people at the exact moments I needed them—not because they knew what I was carrying, but because He did.

I learned something important that week. I learned that I could feel devastation without being destroyed by it. That I could obey without fully understanding. That I could grieve without abandoning myself.

And that I could walk through something that terrified me and come out steadier on the other side.

When my daughter came home, I didn't rush us back into normal. I chose rest. I chose softness. I chose safety.

It snowed that morning—the first snow of a new chapter. And as we sat together, I realized something had shifted.

Fear didn't lead anymore. It only signaled.

And then, I took God's hand and kept going.

Something in me knew this then—I could survive what used to undo me.

CHAPTER 32

Walking, Releasing, Becoming

I'm taking a walk today before I write, because my body needs to move while my heart sorts itself out. There is a lot happening—beautiful things, hard things, and holy things all tangled together—and I can feel how real this season is in my chest.

Yesterday was 1/11 That felt like a bookmark between who I was and who I'm becoming. I could feel it—that subtle, electric sense that something has shifted. I don't know exactly what's coming, but I know I'm standing in a new doorway. God is rearranging my terrain. I am in the middle of a miracle, even if I can't see all of it yet.

There's excitement in me.

There's momentum.

There's also fear.

I'm proud of myself for the way I've been showing up. I joined a breathwork session with my new somatic coach, and I could feel how right it was. I followed the nudge. I didn't overthink it. I let my body and intuition lead. That alone feels like proof that I'm not the same woman I was even a year ago.

I'm ready for guidance. I'm ready to be supported. I'm ready to grow into the next version of myself instead of shrinking to survive.

So, today I'm walking.

I'm breathing. I'm letting the truth exist without forcing it to resolve yet.

I can hold excitement and fear at the same time.

I can be becoming and still grieving.

I can trust God while also advocating for myself and my daughter.

This season is real.

It's tender.

And it's sacred.

I don't know exactly how everything will unfold—but I know I am not lost. I am moving. I am listening. I am choosing myself. And somehow, even in the middle of the unknown, I can feel something good is being built.

I woke up on a Monday morning in 2026 feeling something unfamiliar in my body: forward motion.

Not urgency.

Not pressure.

Not the tight, braced energy I used to mistake for motivation. That is so new to me.

Movement. For a long time, simply moving forward had felt impossible. Grief had frozen me. Fear had stalled me. My nervous system had stayed on high alert, always scanning for what might break next.

But this morning was different. I wasn't rushing. I wasn't hiding. I was awake—present—and meeting what was in front of me without panic. That alone felt miraculous.

The woman standing here didn't arrive by accident. She was forged.

This month marked three years since I'd stopped speaking to my mother. Three years since the story I thought I knew about my life had cracked open and demanded to be reexamined. Three years of therapy, EMDR, bilateral work, somatic healing, and hormone work—the slow, holy labor of untangling trauma that had lived in my body long before I had language for it.

It was the hardest work I've ever done.

And the most sacred.

There was something symbolic about this particular morning, the day after January 11—the day I decided to pull Maddie from public school—that quiet marker between who I had been and who I was becoming. I could feel it in my chest: grief and gratitude living side by side, fear braided with faith. I wasn't arriving at certainty. I was stepping through a threshold.

That same day, I sat down with my daughter and began homeschooling her.

Writing that still feels surreal.

The curriculum had arrived over the weekend—creative writing, drawing, and history. Simple materials that felt like possibility wrapped in cardboard. There was no rush to get it right. No pressure to replicate what we had left behind. This season wasn't about achievement. It was about safety. Curiosity. Learning how to trust ourselves again.

And if I'm honest, what scared me most wasn't logistics or schedules.

It was worthiness.

There was a part of me that quietly wondered if I was capable enough. Smart enough. Qualified enough. A part that had spent a lifetime believing other people were more equipped to lead, teach, and decide. Believing that I could support, but not be *the one*.

My whole life, I would have said no to something like this.

But the truth is, homeschooling isn't about proving intelligence or perfection. It's about meeting a child where she is—emotionally, developmentally, always gently. And when I looked at it through that lens, something shifted. This choice wasn't reckless. It was aligned. It was what Maddie's nervous system needed. What our life needed.

Still—letting go of the idea that someone else would always be watching over her, guiding her, and providing structure brought its own fear. What about socialization? What about support? What about getting it wrong?

And underneath all of that, the deeper fear surfaced: *What if I'm not enough?*

I sat with that belief long enough to see it for what it was. BS. Not in an angry way—but in a healed way. The kind of clarity that doesn't argue anymore. The kind that simply says: That story doesn't belong here.

In fact, I have a quiet sense that I'm going to excel at this. Not because I'm perfect—but because I'm present. Because I care. Because I'm not trying to mold my daughter into something she's not. I'm protecting her while she becomes who she is.

There's a quiet knowing that comes when you realize you're living the reason you're writing.

If I don't tell this story, people won't believe it's possible—that someone can survive childhood trauma, betrayal, gaslighting, addiction in the family, religious confusion, and a marriage that slowly collapsed... and still come out soft. Still faithful. Still standing.

I want people to know that God works for good—not just for those who had tidy faith journeys, but for those who were lost, confused, and surviving with nervous systems wired for danger. Even when love was conditional. Even when survival was mistaken for devotion.

That was me.

Healing didn't come from pretending any of it was easy. It came from telling the truth. From letting myself feel grief and anger and exhaustion without rushing past them. From surrender—not as defeat, but as release.

Surrender is my word for 2026.

Not giving up.

Giving over.

For most of my life, control was my survival skill. If I could manage the narrative—my feelings, other people's reactions, and the outcome—I could stay safe. So, surrendering control doesn't come naturally to me. It requires trust. It requires believing that God is working, even when I'm not gripping the wheel.

I'm learning to let my core lead instead of fear.

And I can feel the difference now.

But that's not who I am anymore.

I'm finishing my manuscript.

I'm homeschooling my daughter.

I'm walking into new business, new retreats, and new purpose—calmly.

And when I pause long enough to really take that in, I realize something extraordinary: I'm not just surviving my life anymore. I'm building it.

And that feels like the beginning of everything.

I know I didn't arrive here overnight. Years of healing came before this—therapy, EMDR, learning how to understand my body and trust what it was telling me.

By the time everything shifted I was ready to see it clearly—and to respond differently.

I know I couldn't have made all these hard decisions without the years of healing that came before it—therapy, EMDR, nervous system work, and the slow building of trust with God. That work gave me the ability to surrender. To cry. To feel. To lament without collapsing. My therapist once told me lament is a form of worship, and I held onto that like an anchor. I wasn't falling apart in my tears. I was worshiping in them.

The in-between where the old life is gone but the new one hasn't fully formed yet. And still, even there, I could feel Him. Not loudly. Not theatrically. Quietly. Steadily. Like a whisper that didn't leave.

Grief can make you feel like you're on an island, unseen in the waves. But then I'd remember: I have God. And God had already been arranging support around me—chosen family, women who stood with me, therapists, encouragers, mother-figures, and friends, who held my hand through the parts I didn't think I could survive. They helped get me to the edge of the decision.

I didn't know exactly what God was doing, but I knew something big was stirring inside me. I didn't know how I would share it yet, but I knew I would. So, I did what I've learned to do: sit, breathe, allow, receive, and trust. I stopped looking for a dramatic sign and started trusting the quiet evidence—peace growing in my heart like a garden only He can plant. Not shallow happiness. Not applause. Not external wealth. Peace. The kind that changes the atmosphere of a home.

I had originally pictured retreat in a full house—women, laughter, healing, and sisterhood. And when the women I hoped would come couldn't, it broke my heart more than I expected. I really thought at least one of them would be with me. But instead of bitterness, I felt disappointment… and a strange increase of faith. Their absence shifted me into something else. Not failure. Not rejection. A sabbatical, maybe. A holy quiet. So, I went anyway. Alone. And I decided I would worship, seek, and listen.

Maddie was my grounding force through all of it. She was my anchor—my reminder of what matters most. Her emotional safety became the center of my decisions, not an afterthought. I walked her into school. Talked with her counselor. Sat with her and made room for feelings without rushing to fix them. I kept checking in. I kept learning. And I felt proud—not in a "look at me" way, but in a quiet way that said, "We're doing something different. We're building safety."

Then came the first weekend I sent her to her dad's new place. And what surprised me wasn't that it was hard—it was that I was calm. God gave me strength to send my daughter off with blessings and love. That alone was a miracle.

I didn't grow up receiving blessings. I received anger. Manipulation. Control. Shame. But I made a vow: I will not pass that down. I am a chain-breaker mom. I will keep breaking the chains that bound me, so my daughter can walk in freedom.

And here's something that still makes me smile through tears: Maddie's favorite day of the week became therapy. What eleven-year-old says that? But she did. And to me, that meant everything. It meant we were building something safer than what I'd inherited. Something sacred.

I didn't just have grief days. I had grief hours.

The waves came spontaneously—sometimes several times a day. And when they came, I let them. I didn't force anything. I didn't try to be strong or push through. I let my heart feel what it was actually carrying. And it hurt. It really hurt. There's no way around that truth.

No one wants to feel that kind of pain. I understand why people avoid it. But I allowed myself to cry—not in a dramatic, unraveling way, but in a quiet, releasing way. A letting-go way. Those cries didn't fix anything. They didn't suddenly make me "better." But they released something. And every time, I noticed the same thing: I felt a little lighter afterward, even though I was still very much in the process.

Grief is strange like that. Some days, you cry hard, and other days, you don't cry at all—and then you wonder what's wrong with you. Nothing is wrong. It's just grief doing what grief does. Moving. Shifting. Coming and going.

I don't think I'm done grieving. But I do know this: I grieved a lot. And that mattered.

What helped me cope wasn't numbing or distraction—it was care. Rest. Water. Letting my body slow down. Massage to help my nervous system release what words could not. Somatic care. Therapeutic touch. Reflexology. I believe wholeheartedly in tending to the body while the heart heals.

Trauma and grief live in the body, and they deserve gentleness there.

Allowing myself to feel—without judgment, without rushing—was one of the most important things I've ever done for my healing.

I started living by a different kind of wisdom in that season: pause and respond. I held Proverbs 15:1 close: "A gentle answer turns away wrath." I listened to God, to Maddie, to her therapist, and even to the voices around her that were paying attention.

When multiple voices pointed to the same truth—that Maddie felt uncomfortable and unsafe during stays at her dad's—that alignment didn't feel like coincidence. It felt like confirmation. And I made my decision: Maddie's emotional well-being comes first. I would communicate with clarity and grace, document what mattered, involve her therapist as needed, and keep God at the center.

When I came home from Broken Bow in September, something in me felt different. I felt overwhelming excitement, peace, and joy. I didn't feel anxious. Just calm and strangely lit up for what was coming. I didn't even know what it was yet. I just had glimpses—like God was letting me see the outline of the life ahead without forcing me to hold the whole blueprint.

I grieved my husband. I grieved our life. Maybe not fully. Maybe there was more to come. But I had cried devastation-tears, and I chose that. I chose to feel. I chose healing. I chose to get closer to Him.

And when I posted stories, I could already hear the comments people always make: Did you have the whole place to yourself? Was it still a retreat? How many women were there? Something inside me wanted to shrink, to explain, to defend, to prove my worthiness. But I didn't do that anymore. I started treating everything as data—not judgment. I evaluated myself, not the noise. I watched what triggered me and what didn't. I learned discernment has a relationship with triggers, but it doesn't belong to them.

I knew my original vision hadn't happened the way I'd expected. But it wasn't a "never." It was a "not yet." God wanted me to heal first. To become steady first. To accept the truth first. To build a home with pure love, laughter, and responses instead of reactions, with God in every conversation. To embody healing, not just talk about it in a therapy room. That's what I was becoming.

Even the airport chaos on the way home became proof—delays, gate changes, rebooking. And I noticed my body. My mind. My reactions. The old me would've spiraled. The current me stayed regulated. That's how redemption shows up: in the small moments. If it's not good, He's not done.

On an evening stroll back on my dirt roads after my September retreat, it hit me again: my standards had raised, my boundaries were bolder, and my peace was solidifying. I could feel Jesus carrying me—like freedom in the breeze, like wide-open space. I didn't know exactly where He was taking me, but I knew there were blessings there.

And I also knew there were hard conversations ahead, especially with Maddie's dad. I wasn't looking forward to them. But this version of me was different. I still felt fear, but fear wasn't driving the bus anymore. The old part of me was present, but she wasn't dominant. My core got to lead.

I remember a small moment with Maddie—one of those ordinary holy ones. We talked about reacting versus responding. She asked what it meant, and I gave her a simple example: responding is when you pause before you speak; reacting is when the automated system fires without thought.

That conversation landed in me like a marker. I am cycle-breaking in the tiny moments. Not because I said one perfect thing once, but because I keep showing my daughter what safety looks like. Over and over again.

And at some point in all of it, I realized what I couldn't have understood three years prior: healing isn't a dramatic finish line. It's a thousand quiet choices. It's pausing. It's listening. It's protecting. It's letting God rewire what survival taught you was "normal."

So, I kept saying yes.

CHAPTER 33

Joy as a Healing Practice - not a Reward

For a long time, I thought joy was something you earned after healing—a reward once everything was figured out. But healing taught me something different. Joy is not the finish line. It's part of the work.

Travel, shared experiences, laughter, small rituals, and the ordinary moments Maddie and I build together aren't escapes from healing—they are how my nervous system learns safety in real time.

Naming joy as a healing practice changed how I live. I don't postpone joy until life feels stable or complete. I practice it daily, intentionally, and without guilt.

Joy doesn't minimize pain or bypass grief. It creates space alongside it. This is the life I'm choosing now: one where joy is woven into my days, not saved for someday.

CHAPTER 34

Safe Expansion

When I went on my first retreat with Raina, it felt so different from anything I had experienced before. In her presence, my nervous system noticed it before my brain did. I felt calmer almost instantly, and that alone told me something mattered here.

I had never met her in person. I only knew her online, loosely from online—back in the Beachbody days. She wasn't someone I followed closely, but whenever she showed up on my screen, I was always intrigued.

She carried this quiet confidence and grounded authenticity that felt real. She wasn't trying to impress any one—she just was. I remember thinking she was a badass—in the softest way. Shaved head. Tattoos. This unmistakable light inside her that felt earned, not curated.

It's funny how we think we know people because we see them online. I laugh about that now, because I know people probably think they know me, too. And yet, sometimes that instinct is right. Sometimes, your body recognizes truth before words ever do.

I remember noticing that she had disappeared from social media for a while. When she resurfaced, something about her felt different. Deeper. Quieter. Healed in a way that wasn't loud. She had written a book, and the moment I saw it, I felt that familiar pull. Not urgency. Just a soft, persistent knowing. I read it, and I was immediately drawn to her story, her honesty, and the way she shared without performing. It felt safe.

So, when I saw she was hosting retreats—writing, healing, and horses—I didn't overthink it. I just knew I needed to go.

The first retreat was in Colorado. It was a writing and healing retreat, held in a beautiful home with five or six other women from completely different walks of life. Every one of us was there for the same reason: to breathe, to be still, to heal, and to reconnect with ourselves. We journaled. We spent time with the horses. We talked. We rested. There was no pressure to become anything other than what we already were.

Healing with horses is something I don't know how to fully explain—unless you've experienced it. Being barefoot. Being present. Letting your body lead instead of your mind. It was powerful and grounding and gentle all at once. I loved every minute of that retreat.

She hosted another retreat later that year in Marble Falls, Texas. I went again without hesitation. That one was even deeper. I connected with so many women during that retreat, but there was one moment I'll never forget.

Later that year, I went to another retreat in Marble Falls Texas. It was even deeper. I connected with so many women, but there was 1 moment I'll never forget.

It was my birthday—December 8, 2024. We were driving to the airport. Raina was driving, and there were three of us crammed in the back seat, suitcases everywhere. I was sitting next to Emily.

In that moment, I saw a text come through from my mother. A birthday message. And instantly, my heart sank.

I didn't know what to do with it. It hurt. It brought up so much pain all at once.

And then, God whispered, *Emily is right there.*

So, I leaned my head over and rested it on her shoulder.

Emily—who was quietly walking through a heavy life change of her own—held me without hesitation. No questions. No fixing. Just presence.

I remember it so clearly. God had placed exactly the right person next to me in that moment. Someone gentle. Someone safe. Someone who could hold me when I didn't have the words.

That's what God does. He meets us right where we are. He doesn't always remove the pain—but He never leaves us alone in it.

After those retreats, Raina and I stayed connected. We became fast friends. She was a mentor to me in ways she probably doesn't even realize. When she and her fiancé were moving to Georgia, she texted me and asked—almost casually—if she could borrow our barn for Caesar and Joey while they passed through.

It was an immediate yes.

I didn't even know how I was going to make it work yet. I just knew I would. Opening my space to them felt natural—right, even joyful. I had connected deeply with Caesar in Colorado—bareback, slow, present. He has the kind of soul you feel more than you see. That old, gentle wisdom. Healing through horses is something that stays with you.

They came through in January 2025, and it was absolutely freezing. Truly freezing. Like frozen-tundra freezing. We laughed about it nonstop. I think it became a running joke that they'd never come back unless I promised Kansas wouldn't feel like the Arctic next time.

They stayed just one night, but it meant so much to me. I made little gifts for Raina, because that's my love language. I felt honored to be part of their journey—to support them as they moved into their new life together. It brought me so much joy to be able to give in that way, freely, without obligation or fear.

That season with Raina—those retreats, that friendship, that trust—showed me what safe expansion looks like. What it feels like to grow without pressure. To be guided without being controlled. To heal without having to prove anything.

It was another way God rebuilt my support system—slowly, intentionally, with people who could meet me emotionally, spiritually, and honestly.

Those retreats were so incredibly different than anything I had experienced before, because they included horses. In Texas, we even did yoga with the horses—lying on them bareback, rubbing on them, breathing with them. In Colorado, we were up close and personal with the horses in a way that felt intimate and grounding.

I had no idea how healing horses could be. I'd heard people say it before, but I didn't truly understand until I experienced it myself.

I've always loved horses. I remember them from when I was very little. My Grandpa Smith was around them a lot—

raising them, training them, breaking them. Horses always scared me a little, but I loved riding and being around them anyway.

Over the years, though, I noticed my nervous system becoming more uneasy, more cautious, and less comfortable around them. That is part of the reason why I wanted to go to these retreats. I knew I had always had a connection with horses—their energy, their presence, and how majestic they are. The way they hold and release energy, the way they receive without judgment. It's something you really can't explain. You have to experience it.

There was a moment in Colorado when it was just me on Cesar, bareback. I was carrying so much shame and hurt and betrayal—betrayal trauma that was still incredibly painful—and I left it with him. I lay there, completely bareback, trusting this massive, beautiful animal—a thousand, maybe two thousand pounds—and I was overcome with emotion.

Raina was talking to me softly, and I closed my eyes, felt the wind on my skin, breathed deeply, and allowed myself to be fully there. I couldn't believe my body could do that. I couldn't believe I was able to feel that safe.

I cried real, authentic tears. I connected with Cesar—this beautiful old soul—and it felt like he took my pain from me. I left it there with him. It was heartbreaking and healing at the same time. He was such a good boy. Truly. He held my pain without resistance.

That experience changed me. Horses are gentle giants, and the energy they carry and share is unreal. It's sacred. I genuinely believe they are one of God's healing instruments.

The retreat in Texas was just as powerful in a different way. I stayed in a yurt at the ranch, and it felt so good to say, "I'm doing this. I'm going."

I allowed myself to feel nervous and excited at the same time. I gave myself permission to heal however I could. Those retreats weren't about dipping a toe in—they were about immersion. Being in nurturing, safe environments. Journaling. Sitting still. Laughing. Dancing. Making reels. Letting joy exist alongside grief.

It felt empowering to choose myself in that way—to seek out connection, healing, and safety instead of staying frozen. I had so much fun, and I felt proud of myself for going. Those experiences reminded me that healing doesn't always come from talking—sometimes it comes from being held, breathing, and letting your body remember what safety feels like.

PART SIX

A HAVEN OF HER OWN

CHAPTER 35

Costa Rica: A Turning Point

And then, of course, when Raina told me about Costa Rica, I was immediately intrigued. I never imagined being able to go to Costa Rica—especially with someone I knew, trusted, and felt safe with. The way she talked about it made it sound like a trip of a lifetime. It felt exciting and expansive and just a little unreal. So, I said, screw it and I booked it.

I went—and it changed my entire life.

I loved every single minute. I miss every soul from that trip, and I want to go back right now. I'm not exaggerating when I say it was one of the most incredible, exotic, dream-level experiences I've ever had. Truly unreal.

The only thing that was a little challenging for my nervous system was the go-go-go pace—and honestly, that's not a critique. It was just something I noticed in my body.

We rode horses through the jungle by moonlight. No joke. Actual moonlight. Galloping through the jungle on horseback like something out of a movie. It was wild and freeing and so much fun. The women were incredible.

I felt deeply connected—to the people, to the ocean, to nature, and to my own body. I surfed. I fell. I got board rash on my stomach. I got back up. I learned. I laughed. And I stood up on the board. I was so proud of myself.

Being there helped me grow in ways I didn't expect. Not through talking, but through doing. Through trying. Through trusting my body. Through letting myself be alive. I've already looked up the dates again. That's how good it was.

If anyone ever asks me about it, I say the same thing every time: it's a well-run, intentional experience, and I trust the women who lead it. I love them. I cheer for them. My heart holds them.

But here's the part I didn't know yet.

Costa Rica wasn't just a retreat.

It was clarity.

It stripped away the noise I didn't even realize I was still carrying the performing, the anticipating, the subtle racing I had learned to live inside of.

And underneath all of that I met myself again.

Not a new version. Not someone I had to become. Just me—without the pressure, without the scanning, without the need to get it right.

I didn't go looking for answers. My body already had them. I went because something in me knew I needed to remember who I was when I wasn't shrinking, explaining, or bracing for impact.

There was a version of me that surfaced there—steady, alive, curious, and at ease. Not performing. Not surviving. Just present. And once I felt that in my body, I couldn't unfeel it. That was the shift. Not a decision I forced… but a knowing I couldn't override any more.

My body had experienced something true and so freeing—and once it did everything else started to feel out of alignment.

That's the part no one tells you about healing: once your nervous system experiences safety, it stops negotiating with fear.

Costa Rica didn't convince me to leave.

It simply made it impossible to keep pretending.

I remember how excited my body felt when I boarded the plane. Light. Free. Almost giddy in a way I hadn't felt in years. As we flew over the mountains, I looked out the window and felt something lift—like all the grief, the heaviness, and the constant bracing I carried at home couldn't follow me up there. My nervous system felt open. Curious. Ready.

When we arrived at the house, I was in awe immediately. From the living space, you could see straight into the jungle—layers of green, with movement everywhere, and life pulsing all around us. It was wild and grounding at the same time. Majestic. Alive. I felt deeply loved in that moment—by nature, by beauty, and by whatever force had carried me there. I remember thinking, *I can't believe I get to experience this.*

Then, I met the women.

We all came from different places, different lives, and different stories—but when we sat together in that first circle, I felt an immediate sense of safety. Seen. Held. Allowed to receive and to give.

Raina guided us through journaling and sharing, and it was everything I didn't know how to ask for but deeply needed. It felt aligned—with my heart, my healing, and my faith. I remember thinking, *I want to do this again tomorrow. And again, after that.*

As the women shared pieces of their lives, I could feel God weaving threads between us. I wasn't just meeting them—I was meant to meet them here. During one session, as I listened to another woman who had the most beautiful Australian accent talk about her mother, something in me cracked open. I felt deeply connected to her—her accent, her light, and the familiarity of her pain. From that moment on, that surfboard sister held a permanent place in my heart. My freckled sister. A fellow cycle-breaker. We still talk about meeting up one day and getting a tattoo together—a symbol of chains broken, of childhoods we never deserved, of sisters who found each other anyway.

And it wasn't just her. When each woman spoke, I felt that same quiet confirmation: *You are exactly where you're supposed to be. These women will help carry you through what's coming next.*

There were women there from all over the world—each carrying her own story, her own healing, her own becoming. I remember this beautiful Italian woman and another incredible soul Mona. Something about them that drew me in immediately. Their presence felt soft, open, and real in a way I hadn't experienced in a long time, or maybe ever. It wasn't just what they said—While they were. You could feel the kindness in them. The authenticity. It was like it was woven into everything—Into their words, their tone, even the way they looked at people.

They had done their own work. You could feel it. They had found their way back to themselves—In different ways, through their own paths—but it showed. And being around that… it did something to me. Listening to their stories was powerful, but even more than that, it was the connection between all of us. It was pure, easy and safe.

There were also two younger girls there that I had connected with right away. Something about the way they saw me—it touched a part of me I hadn't fully been connected to in a while. They looked at me like I was safe, like I was steady… like a mama figure. And I realized how much I loved that. How natural it felt to hold that space, to care, to be present with them and just see each other fully.

The most healing moments weren't structured or planned—they just happened. On the beach, riding horses, standing in the ocean, sitting in silence, or wrapped up in long hugs that lasted just a little longer than usual. There was a depth to those moments that I can't fully explain, only feel when I think back on them now. These women changed me in ways I'm still uncovering. Their stories, their presence, their hearts—they've stayed with me. And I know they always will. I didn't realize then how deeply that connection would stay with me.

One of the most powerful experiences there was surfing—something I had never done in my life. It felt foreign. Scary. Completely outside my comfort zone. But I tried it. And I got up. I faced the fear and did the thing anyway.

My surf coach, Vero, was pure kindness. I trusted her immediately. She guided me gently, patiently, like she understood my nervous system was learning something brand new. I felt clumsy, like a fish out of water, trying to coordinate my body while waves moved beneath me in this vast, beautiful ocean that felt both exhilarating and terrifying at the same time.

There were moments when I waited out in the water alone, holding onto my board, no waves coming. Just stillness. I remember talking to God out there—floating, breathing, and listening. He didn't rush me. He didn't push. The message was simple: *Enjoy this. Let your body learn something new. Let it rupture and repair. Let this rewire what no longer serves you.*

So, I let the ocean regulate me. I listened to the sounds. I breathed. I rested right there in the middle of something unfamiliar.

And then there was a moment I'll never forget. A man named Mariano helped run the retreat. He was always nearby—supportive, kind, and steady. He took photos and videos of us surfing, while cheering us on. As I was preparing to ride a wave, Vero pointed out that Mariano was out there filming me. She told me to focus on him. To ride the wave toward him.

And boy, I surely did.

As I stood up and rode that wave, something shifted. I consciously released the old survival wiring—the part of me that would normally think about how I looked, whether I was doing it right, and how the image would turn out. Instead, I just felt the wave. The motion. The joy. I let myself be seen without performing.

And that was new for me. Not being watched and adjusting … not scanning for how I was being received. Just existing in my body—fully present, without editing myself. I didn't realize how much of my life had been lived that way until I felt the absence of it.

As I got closer, I saw Mariano watching me—fully present, cheering, and capturing the moment simply because it mattered. And suddenly, I was overcome with emotion. Real, embodied tears. Gratitude. Safety. Being witnessed without expectation.

I rode that wave all the way in, crying, and when I reached him, I said, "Thank you"—not just for the video, but for being there. For witnessing me.

I paddled back out to Vero and told her what had just happened. I don't know if she fully understood my words—her English was limited—but she understood my tears. She understood the release. She saw the weight lift.

That moment stayed with me. It still does.

Costa Rica wasn't just beautiful. It wasn't just fun or adventurous or healing in theory. It changed my body. My nervous system. My sense of what was possible.

And when I came home, I knew.

I knew I couldn't go back to shrinking. I knew I couldn't pretend anymore. That trip marked the division point. So much was changing, internally and externally, and it was such a blessing to be able to find so much beauty in the most incredible place on Earth.

Costa Rica wasn't just a retreat.

It was clarity. It stripped away the noise I didn't know I was still carrying. The performing. They anticipating. The subtle bracing I had learned to live inside of.

And underneath all of that… I was able to meet myself again.

It showed me who I was when I was free—and what I could no longer unsee. And I know this for sure: I will go back.

I noticed the shift as soon as I came home. My body was tired, but my nervous system was calm in a way I wasn't used to yet.

Seeing my daughter felt easy. Natural. Grounding.

But something in me had changed. Not dramatic. Just... different.

I didn't have language for it yet. I just knew I wasn't the same. It felt like I was standing between two worlds—no longer who I had been, but not fully settled into who I was becoming.

Part of me was still in Costa Rica—still open, still breathing deeply, still remembering what safety felt like.

And then I was back in my kitchen, back in the familiar rhythms of my life. The contrast was quiet but undeniable.

In Costa Rica, my nervous system wasn't bracing. I wasn't scanning or performing. I felt calm in my body in a way I hadn't felt in years.

Back home, my body slipped into old patterns without asking:

Don't set anything off.

Do everything right.

Stay small.

Keep the peace.

It wasn't conscious. It was familiar.

But now, it didn't fit the same way.

Something in me had started resisting.

I couldn't unknow what safety felt like.

What shifted wasn't my circumstances—it was a promise. A direct promise my heart had made with God. I knew it distinctly. I knew it with every fiber of my being. I just didn't know *how* I was going to keep it yet.

So, I stopped trying to see the big picture.

I chose gentle intention instead—one step at a time—trusting I would see Him guiding me as I moved.

Costa Rica didn't give me answers. It gave me something more honest than answers.

It gave me contrast.

A clear, undeniable difference between who I was when I felt safe and who I had been trying to be just to survive.

What it gave me was something deeper—an extra layer of love and support from God, through the humans He placed in my life. It allowed my nervous system to integrate healing in a way I hadn't experienced before. I was able to try new things, feel supported, feel validated, and experience safety in my body—not as an idea, but as a lived reality.

And once my nervous system experienced that level of safety, I couldn't ignore what it was telling me anymore.

When Healing Makes Staying Impossible

The more healed I got, the harder it became to pretend I was someone I wasn't anymore.

The more healed I got, the harder it became to lie about what I already knew.

The more healed I got, the harder it became to believe there was any solution other than leaving.

My body wasn't being dramatic—it was being honest.

I had learned what safety felt like, and I couldn't unknow it.

Healing didn't make the situation worse.

It made the truth unavoidable.

Something was different because I actually went.

Something was different because I didn't overexplain.

Something was different because I trusted myself.

Something was different because my body felt calm about the decision, even if my mind knew what was coming next wouldn't be easy.

I had stood up for myself—quietly, internally—and once I did that, I couldn't pretend not to know.

You Don't Have to Prove This Was Real

CHAPTER 36

Standing Between Two Worlds

I remember trying to capture everything—pictures, videos, proof that it happened. And then God stopped me.

He reminded me I don't have to document moments to validate them anymore. I don't have to fill my camera roll to prove my life is real. The little girl who did that was surviving. I get to live now.

The memories don't need evidence. They're already imprinted.

Real life confirming my truth:

In the weeks that followed Costa Rica, everything blurred together in a way I'd never experienced before. Days ran into each other. Sometimes, even hours did. I found myself opening my calendar just to anchor my brain—to give myself a visual sense of time, so my nervous system could feel a little safer.

When I look back now, I can see why. It had been over a month since a conversation I knew I would never forget.

I remember finally telling my husband how emotionally disconnected and alone I had been feeling. I tried to explain how deeply I was craving connection, presence, and care within our marriage.

We talked for a long time that day. I explained that I had been doing deep work on myself—going to therapy, being vulnerable, trying to understand my patterns, my nervous system, and the ways I wanted to grow.

And in that conversation, he admitted he had been unwilling to fully meet me there.

That honesty mattered. Painful as it was, it gave me clarity."

I left that conversation emotionally exhausted, but also aware of something I could no longer ignore. I'd spent my entire life choosing what was familiar to my nervous system. Overcompensating. Ignoring what my body and heart were telling me. Repeating patterns that began long before adulthood ever arrived.

And for the first time, it was all starting to make sense. That day changed something permanently.

A few days earlier, I'd mentioned wanting to go to Costa Rica. A retreat. Something that felt life-giving and necessary. Instead of support, I was met with anger. Accusations. Being told I was disrespecting our marriage for even considering it.

My husband wasn't happy for me.

He wasn't curious.

He wasn't supportive.

And something in me finally stopped bending. For the first time, I allowed myself to acknowledge that something in our marriage had to change.

It wasn't about punishment, anger, or giving up. I simply knew I could not continue carrying the emotional weight of the relationship alone. I wanted healing, honesty, accountability, and growth—and I knew both people had to be willing to move toward those things together.

The following weeks were heavy. I was stepping into a life I hadn't planned—but, deep down, I knew it was right. In the middle of it all, Maddie and I still took our trip. It was hard and beautiful at the same time.

I carried so much grief with me—and still chose to go. Still chose to create memories. Still chose presence. I'm so proud of myself for that.

When we came home, nothing had changed.

The routines were intact.

The distance remained.

The silence was loud.

And I finally understood something I couldn't unknow: people don't just tell you who they are—they show you.

I could keep lying to myself. Or I could get radically honest.

I cried more in those weeks than I ever had. And instead of breaking me, it softened something open. I reached out to my safe people. I let myself be held in ways I hadn't allowed before.

One night, while crying on the phone with a friend, I saw a butterfly—big and bright—dancing right in front of me. Later, a cardinal crossed my path. Gentle reminders that I wasn't alone. That I was being carried.

I even called Mama B. We talked for nearly an hour. She reminded me that marriage requires communication. That life is short. That Maddie deserves a happy mom. That I deserve happiness.

I told her the truth I rarely said out loud: that I have no blood family. No parents. No siblings. And that this felt terrifying.

And yet—somehow—I was surrounded.

That's the miracle I can't ignore.

Even in my loneliest moments, God was meeting me through people.

Through signs.

Through clarity.

Through courage I didn't know I had.

I wasn't falling apart.

I was finally telling the truth.

CHAPTER 37

Inheritance, Wealth, and Safety

Inheritance feels beautiful to me now.

For most of my life, that word scared me. It felt heavy, conditional—almost transactional. It felt like something you could lose if you didn't perform correctly or say the right thing or stay small enough to be tolerated.

Now, inheritance feels different in my body.

Now, inheritance feels like safety—something I am intentionally creating and passing down to my daughter.

The survival patterns I inherited taught me that love and safety could feel inconsistent. That safety was fragile. That love could be withdrawn. That affection often came with strings attached. Love didn't feel like something you could fully rest in. It felt like something you had to earn, manage, or protect.

That kind of inheritance wires a nervous system for vigilance, not peace.

Emotional wealth, on the other hand, looks completely different.

Emotional wealth looks like being my daughter's safe person. It looks like giving her emotional maturity—language for her feelings, space for her experiences, and permission to be human without fear. Emotional wealth looks like soft mornings, not startling her nervous system awake with chaos or sarcasm disguised as humor.

It looks like honoring her emotions instead of minimizing them. It looks like teaching her that conflict is part of life—and that rupture can be followed by repair and rest.

Wealth is not money first.

Wealth is safety first.

Wealth is nurturing the nervous system so it can breathe, trust, and grow.

That understanding changed everything for me. I started to understand this long before I had language for it.

My mother's actions often appeared generous or involved, but something about them felt different in my body. The motive underneath her behavior was about needing to be seen, needing validation, needing attention—not about connection or care. Even when something was presented as help, I often walked away feeling emotionally responsible for her, instead of cared for, myself.

I didn't fully understand this until after I started therapy.

I noticed how, when I went to her house, I'd feel something tighten in my chest. Conversations never moved forward—they looped. Every attempt at calm communication ended with condemnation instead of encouragement. I often left those conversations feeling corrected, misunderstood, or smaller than when I entered them. My body knew something was off long before my mind could explain it.

Now, when I'm around someone whose motive is manipulative, performative, or conditional, I feel it immediately. I don't need proof. I don't need a pattern. My body knows. It feels awful. And I don't care how impressive, accomplished, or well-liked someone is, if I can feel that motive, I'm out. Truly, I'm done and won't partake.

When motive is loving, my body feels safe. My nervous system softens. That difference matters to me now more than almost anything else.

Reparenting doesn't happen in big moments.

It happens on regular Tuesdays.

It looks like slowing down when I notice myself moving too fast. It looks like catching my brain when it runs ahead of my body and choosing to bring us back into the present. It looks like grace—for myself and for my daughter.

I stop myself now from doing things that aren't true to me.

For years, my nervous system ran on automatic. I would adjust the environment before I even checked in with myself—shutting blinds, dimming lights, rearranging my needs—because that's what keeping the peace had always required. I didn't choose it consciously. My body just knew how to protect itself by anticipating someone else.

That pattern is no longer in charge.

I also allow my daughter to see emotion. I don't hide tears. I don't pretend I'm unaffected. I used to believe she shouldn't see that—that strength meant containment. Now, I know better. She gets to see that emotions are real, safe, and survivable.

Another important shift: I allow myself to be wrong.

When my daughter tells me something doesn't feel good, I listen. I don't defend. I don't dismiss. I don't overpower. She is allowed to say when something feels unsafe or uncomfortable. That voice matters.

I am teaching her that emotions are part of life—not something to bury or apologize for.

Safety is not optional anymore.

It just isn't.

This is where it stops.

I will not pass this down.

Yes, it has cost me relationships. It has cost me proximity to people I once tried desperately to keep. It has cost me comfort, approval, and the illusion of belonging. It has cost me much of my blood family. It has cost me being misunderstood and judged by people who don't know the work this takes.

But I will not pass this to my daughter.

Not the fear.

Not the conditional love.

Not the survival wiring This is where the line is drawn.

CHAPTER 38

Choosing Safety

God was moving, and I could feel it in my body.

I woke up that morning with a quiet kind of giddiness—the kind that doesn't come from adrenaline, but from deep rest. The kind where your nervous system recognizes something before your mind has language for it. I smiled without trying, because something inside me already knew.

Then it came back to me.

A burst of energy. A wave of joy. A knowing that landed directly in my body. A part of me was still echoing, *I did it. I did it. I did it.* And she was right. She was valid.

I had done something God had been placing on my heart gently, patiently, over time. I had made a vow in this season not to move rashly—to choose everything with gentle intention. And the night before, it had unfolded so quietly, it almost surprised me.

I had tried a few times before and felt stuck. Then, I felt a nudge: *Open your laptop.*

Click. Click. Click.

And there it was—aligned, peaceful, and clear.

I made a decision that would change everything for us.

Maddie could be homeschooled. We were starting in January.

I didn't have everything figured out—and for the first time, I knew I didn't have to. When you allow God into the intimate details of your life, He brings discernment and clarity you didn't even know to ask for. At least, that's been my experience.

As I sat there, I felt deeply seen. Held. Remembered. Not just as a mother, but as His daughter. I felt trusted with something sacred.

Breaking out of the trauma-conditioned version of myself felt exhilarating. December 2025 became a marker—not because everything was solved, but because something had shifted. I was setting up our life differently now. And I wasn't afraid of the unknown anymore.

God goes before me. I had already surrendered. I would follow.

What struck me most was the timing.

This decision came just before Maddie left that negative elementary school environment—the cruelty, the subtle harm, the quiet wounds. Her name written in unkind words on a metal box outside the school building. Scratched out or not, it had been written. And it had hurt her.

I know those children who did that were wounded, too. I know pain gets passed down. But I would not allow my daughter to be collateral damage.

This felt like a bookend moment—not something I rushed toward for meaning, but something God aligned with care. With gentle intention, He had matched what had been stirring in my heart with what my daughter needed for protection.

He even gave it a name.

Haven Learning.

I was creating a place where Maddie's nervous system could breathe. Where learning could be gentle and curious. Where safety came first. Where growth didn't cost her peace.

And as I sat there, breathing deeply, I realized something else: my own nervous system was calmer than it had ever been. I was walking through a divorce I never wanted and never expected—and I wasn't bitter. I was moving forward. Choosing life. Honoring what we deserved.

This was wisdom I couldn't access before. Empowerment rooted in love. Guidance that felt both earned and gifted.

It was all coming together.

There was a moment—quiet, devastating, and unmistakable—when I realized just how much my daughter was carrying.

It wasn't loud. It wasn't dramatic.

But it rearranged everything inside me.

From that day on, protection stopped being a concept and became a calling. I didn't panic. I didn't harden. I simply got clearer.

Healing, I learned, isn't passive. It's watchful. It's responsive. It's the willingness to stay soft while standing guard.

And that kind of love doesn't announce itself—it quietly changes the way you move through the world.

Andrea didn't enter my life out of nowhere. I had seen her before. At some point in the year before everything unraveled, I came across her online. I remember pausing when I saw her—something about the way she carried herself felt different. Soft. Grounded. Safe in a way I didn't yet have language for.

I didn't reach out then. Life kept moving. And soon after, everything at home began to split open.

But later—after the dust started to settle, after I had begun writing this book, and after everything in me was shifting—I felt it again.

A quiet nudge. *Look into her.* And this time, I listened.

I saw that she offered coaching—somatic work, nervous system support, and the kind of care I didn't even realize I needed yet.

And I had this thought, clear as anything: *If I'm going to release something this personal into the world… I need to be supported while I do it.*

This book wasn't just a project. It was the most vulnerable thing I had ever created. And for the first time, I chose not to do something like that alone.

We connected—and I knew almost immediately.

It wasn't forced. It wasn't complicated. It felt like recognition. Like my body exhaled before my mind could catch up.

She became a safe place for me in a season that felt big, exposed, and unfamiliar. When things felt overwhelming… when old patterns tried to resurface… when fear crept in as I got closer to sharing my story—I didn't shut down the way I used to.

I reached out. And that, in itself, was new.

Through her, I experienced tools I had never truly had access to before—somatic practices, mirror work, and learning how to stay present in my body instead of abandoning myself.

Not because I wasn't capable before. But because I wasn't ready.

Now, I was.

Andrea didn't come into my life to fix me. She reflected something back to me at exactly the right time—that I was safe to be seen.

I don't use the word angel lightly, but it's the only one that fits. Not because she came to save me, but because she reflected something sacred back to me at the exact right time.

Before I make any big decision now—especially in business or expansion—I do something I never used to do. I consult my father.

I talk to him. I sit with what he would say. I listen for the quiet knowing in my body. He was always a remarkable judge of character. A wise businessman. A man who understood people.

And when I bring Andrea into that inner conversation, the answer feels clear.

Your father would want this for you.

That realization matters to me more than I can explain. Absorbing his goodness. His discernment. His steadiness—and now knowing he is my biological father, it has become one of the great redemptions of my life.

Andrea didn't create this next season.

She confirmed it.

She represents the shift from healing into stewardship. From surviving into building. From safety found—into safety shared.

And it feels really, really good.

Thank you for staying.

Thank you for holding these words with care.

I never imagined writing a memoir. And now, I can't imagine not telling the truth of this life.

This book wasn't written from bitterness.

It was written from clarity.

From grief.

From love.

I'm still becoming.

Still discerning.

Still learning how to carry what I've been given.

And yes—I have a quiet sense that another book may already be forming.

But for now, this is enough.

Healing doesn't end the story.

It opens it.

And I'm walking forward with gratitude, curiosity, and trust—believing that what's ahead will be met the same way everything else has been: with honesty, courage, and a deep commitment to safety.

CHAPTER 39

The Yellow Butterfly

One summer morning in 2025, I was outside with my coffee while Maddie was still asleep. I was walking the patio, talking to God the way I do now—out loud, honest, and unfiltered. I asked Him for guidance that day. For clarity. For confirmation. I wasn't dramatic about it. I just meant it.

Maddie usually likes to stay in her room in the mornings, but that day, she followed me outside. I noticed it, and I loved it. I love that she sees me caring for myself this way—getting sunlight, noticing God's creatures, and praying. I know it's shaping her, even if she doesn't realize it yet.

We saw a few small butterflies fluttering around while she played with her net. And then, without planning it, I put my hands together and prayed out loud. I told her about the yellow butterfly God had been sending me lately—big, bright, and unmistakable.

I said, "God, will You please show us that yellow butterfly?"

We moved on. Music on. Normal life. And then, just minutes later, Maddie squealed.

"Mommy—*LOOK.*"

I turned, and there it was. The same bright-yellow butterfly, flying up toward the roof right in front of us. I gasped. I fumbled for my phone, trying to capture it, but we didn't get a photo. It disappeared as quickly as it came.

And that was okay.

Because we both saw it.

God didn't just show up for me—He showed up for us. And I felt it settle in my body in a way I can't explain: This is your life now. You chose Me. And I'm with you.

That moment wasn't isolated. It was layered. It was the prayer earlier. Maddie following me outside. The timing. The stillness. The yes to slow down and notice.

God met us there.

And I will never forget it.

CHAPTER 40

What My Body Knows Now

There are things we remember with our minds. And then there are things our bodies remember long before our minds catch up. I didn't know this until healing slowed me down enough to listen.

During a recent deep tissue massage—one of the many that have quite literally kept me alive—the therapist was working in a very specific way. I was lying on my back while she stretched an impacted area by gently pulling and lengthening my neck. It was slow. Intentional. Precise. Her fingertips were steady, patient, and grounded.

And suddenly—without warning—my father appeared.

Not as a thought.

Not as a memory I had to search for.

But as a felt sense.

My body recognized the movement before my brain did.

My father used to do this to me.

I can see it so clearly now...

I'm on the floor of my parents' old house, lying on my back.

My pop—Tomp—would kneel behind me and say, "Hold still. I'm going to pull your neck back." He used his fingertips on the back of my neck and applied pressure in a very specific way—slow, intentional, careful.

He would hold it for a moment, and then, when he released, there was this incredible rush. Tingling. Relief. A sensation so good I remember thinking, *Oh my gosh, this is amazing.*

I remember telling him that and feeling so much relief from my body after he did that simple technique. At the time, it was just a moment.

But now I know… it was an imprint.

That memory has lived in my nervous system for over twenty years.

Lying on that massage table as an adult, I realized something astonishing: that moment with my father taught my body, long before I had language for it, that therapeutic touch matters. That intentional, regulated connection is healing. That my body responds to care. That somatic support isn't indulgent—it's essential.

This wasn't just nostalgia.

This was science meeting lived experience. How incredibly wild is that?

Our bodies remember. That isn't poetic language. It's truth.

And in that realization, I understood something even deeper: my love for therapeutic massage, the way it has become a lifeline for my nervous system, the way it has supported my health again and again—none of that came out of nowhere. It came from God. And it came through my father's hands.

I've carried that goodness with me for decades.

For years, I felt guilty about how much I needed that kind of care. I minimized it. Justified it. Questioned myself. But now I know—those sessions didn't save me despite my story. They saved me because of it. Because my body already knew what safety felt like. Because it had been taught, gently and intentionally, long ago.

That realization alone felt like healing.

And it didn't stop there.

Another memory surfaced—one I've carried for years but never fully understood...

The Claiborne house had a ping-pong room. My dad taught me how to play, and I loved it. I was actually pretty good. We would volley back and forth for long stretches of time. I remember the joy, the competitiveness, the connection. It wasn't just play—it was presence.

But what stands out most now wasn't the game itself.

It was what happened when I missed.

I'd mess up a shot and immediately feel that sharp, sinking feeling—disappointment, frustration, and that split-second sense of failure.

I'd look at him and say, "Do over!"

And he'd say, "Okay."

Over and over again.

I missed more times than I can count. And every time, I asked. And every time, he gave me another chance.

Do over.

What's wild to me is this: I've remembered that moment for most of my life. The words. The feeling. The rhythm of it. But I didn't understand what it meant until now—until healing gave me the capacity to see it clearly.

That's the part that matters.

Because without healing, memory is just memory.

With healing, memory becomes wisdom.

Only now can I see that he was teaching my nervous system something profound:

- You get to try again.
- You're not done because you missed.
- Mistakes aren't the end of connection.

He gave me so many do-overs.

And healing allowed me to finally receive that lesson—not just intellectually, but somatically, emotionally, and spiritually.

This is what I've come to understand: we don't access this kind of awareness without healing. We don't receive the data, the insight, or the meaning behind our lived experiences unless our nervous systems are regulated enough to hold it.

Healing is the vehicle.

Healing is the doorway.

Healing is the way we arrive.

And every person gets to choose how they heal.

For me, healing came through God—and through powerful, practical tools. God was never missing. He was always there. What I added were the supports that allowed me to finally hear Him, feel Him, and connect to my body.

I said yes to therapy.

I said yes to EMDR—deep, intense childhood EMDR that changed everything.

I said yes to talk therapy, somatic therapy, and emotional-intelligence work.

Those tools opened pathways in my brain and body that had been closed for years. They helped me understand where my wounds came from—and, just as importantly, where my goodness lived.

I still remember my therapist telling me, sometime in 2021 or 2022, that I was a "straight-A EMDR student." She laughed when she said it, and I laughed, too—but inside, it meant more than I knew how to explain. My mind followed. My body followed. I stayed with it.

And through that process, my faith didn't disappear.

It emerged.

My therapist used to tell me that it's often the other way around—that people find therapy after faith. For me, therapy helped clear the noise so I could finally hear God.

How cool is that?

Healing gave me access.

Healing gave me language.

Healing gave me understanding.

It allowed me to look back and recognize not just what happened, but how it shaped me, how it protected me, and how it prepared me.

And here's the grace in all of this: understanding these moments doesn't require me to deny the painful ones. I don't have to hold onto the harm to honor the truth. I get to choose which imprints I keep in my body.

I get to release what hurt.

And I get to keep what healed.

That is grace.

There is still healing ahead of me. I know that. There always will be. But that doesn't mean I'm not whole right now. It doesn't mean this season isn't enough. It doesn't mean these pages aren't ready.

Releasing this book feels terrifying because it's honest. Because it's embodied. Because it tells the truth not just about what I survived—but about what sustained me.

And yet, sharing it feels obedient.

God has been whispering this to me clearly: *Release all of it.*

Not just the polished parts.

Not just the pieces people like to highlight.

But the crevices. The nuance. The lived experience.

So, I'm offering this story as it is—messy, beautiful, embodied, and true.

Because maybe someone else's body needs permission to remember goodness, too.

Maybe someone else needs to know that healing is available—in whatever form their body can receive it.

And maybe someone else needs to hear this simple, holy truth:

- ♥ Your body remembers love.
- ♥ Healing helps you understand it.
- ♥ And both matter.

Some lessons arrive through words. Others arrive through the body.

This section holds the lessons my father gave me. Some, I understood right away. Many, I carried quietly for years. And others, I didn't fully receive until healing gave me the capacity to understand them.

These are not polished morals or tidy takeaways.

They are imprints. Moments that lived in my nervous system long before I had language for them.

I return to them now—not to rewrite the past, but to recognize the goodness that was there, the wisdom that stayed with me, and the way God used even small moments to teach my body what care, connection, and grace can feel like.

CHAPTER 41

What Healing Taught Me

If you've made it here—if you've walked through this story with me—then I don't want to just close the book.

I want to leave you with something you can carry.

Not just words. Not just ideas. But things I've lived. Practiced. Fought for. Returned to—again and again.

This is what healing taught me.

1. Take people at face value.

This one changed everything for me.

People will tell you exactly who they are—through what they say, what they do, and what they consistently show you. Not always perfectly. Not always clearly. But it's there.

For so many years, I lived in confusion, because I didn't want to accept what was right in front of me. I would soften it. Rewrite it. Create a different version, so it didn't hurt as much

I would take small moments and stretch them into something hopeful—even when the bigger picture was telling me something completely different.

And that kept me stuck.

At some point in my healing, my therapist said something simple: "Take people at face value."

And it clicked. I realized I didn't need to translate, fix, or reinterpret what someone was showing me. I could just receive it.

Take them at their word.

Take them at their patterns.

Take them at their actions.

It will save you time.

It will save you heartache.

It will save you from abandoning yourself just to make something make sense.

When you stop rewriting people... you start seeing clearly.

2. The answer is healing.

If you're wondering what the answer is—this is what I've come to understand: the answer is healing.

Not a specific method. Not a single path. Not one perfect approach... *Healing*.

There are so many ways to get there. Talk therapy. EMDR. Somatic work. Journaling. Retreats. Travel. Stillness. Safe relationships. Even tools and modalities we don't fully understand yet.

For me, it looked like a blend. Therapy helped me understand. EMDR helped my mind & body process. Somatic work helped my body process. Writing helped me release.

Travel helped me expand. Stillness helped me hear myself.

And through all of it—God.

He was the thread that held everything together. The One who made it sacred. The One who met me in every step I was willing to take.

That's why I'll never tell someone, "This is the way."

But I will say this: You have to be willing to heal. If one way doesn't work, try another. If something doesn't resonate, keep going. There is not one door. There are many.

But the invitation is the same: Step into your healing.

3. Your body knows.

This was something I didn't know how to do for most of my life.

I was so used to listening to everyone else—what they needed, what they expected, what they felt—I didn't even realize I had a voice inside of me. Or if I did… I didn't trust it.

Healing changed that.

Slowly, I started paying attention to the small things. If I was tired—I rested. If something felt off—I paused. If I didn't feel safe—I didn't force myself to stay.

That might sound simple. But for me, it was everything. Because I had spent years overriding myself. Talking myself out of what I felt. Forcing myself to be okay when I wasn't.

The truth is—your body knows. That quiet feeling. That hesitation. That pull.

It's there.

You just might not have been taught how to listen to it yet. But once you do… it will guide you in ways logic never could.

4. The right decision doesn't always feel good.

I used to think, if something was right, it would feel peaceful. Easy. Clear.

But some of the most right decisions I've ever made… felt incredibly hard.

They felt like grief. Like loss. Like uncertainty.

They came with tears. With second-guessing. With moments of wanting to go back just because it was familiar.

But, deep down, I knew. There's a difference between something feeling uncomfortable… and something being wrong.

And healing teaches you how to tell the difference.

Sometimes, the right decision is the one that asks you to choose yourself for the first time. And that can feel unfamiliar. Even painful.

But that doesn't mean it's not right.

5. Sit in stillness

We live in a world full of noise.

Constant input. Constant distraction. Constant movement. And while some of it is beautiful… a lot of it keeps us disconnected from ourselves.

Some of the deepest healing I've experienced didn't come from doing more.

It came from being still.

From sitting with myself.

From journaling.

From being outside.

From letting the noise settle, so I could hear what was underneath it.

Stillness can feel uncomfortable at first—especially if you're used to staying busy. But there is so much clarity waiting there. So much truth. So much peace.

And for me… so much of Him.

6. Your core is God-imprinted.

For most of my life, I lived from my wounds. From survival. From patterns shaped by my environment and everything I had been through.

I didn't know there was a difference between that… and my core.

But there is.

Your core is not your trauma. Your core is not your conditioning. Your core is not the version of you who learned how to survive.

Your core is the part of you that was created by Him.

It's steady. It's grounded. It's honest. It knows.

Healing, for me, was the process of peeling back everything that wasn't truly me—so I could finally live from that place.

That's why I talk about "her." That grounded, clear, steady version of me. That's not something I created. That's something I returned to.

God imprinted that within us. And when you begin to live from that place instead of your wounds… everything changes.

7. Trust yourself.

If there is one thing I will protect for the rest of my life—it's this.

For years, I didn't trust myself. I second-guessed everything. I looked outside of myself for answers. I relied on other people to tell me what was right.

And, in the process... I abandoned myself.

Healing gave that back to me. Slowly. Through practice.

Through pausing. Through listening. Through choosing differently—even when it felt uncomfortable.

And now—I trust myself.

Not perfectly. Not with ego. But with a grounded, steady knowing.

I trust what I feel.

I trust what I sense.

I trust what God is showing me through my life.

And that trust didn't come from thinking. It came from showing myself, over time, that I will listen. That I will respond. That I won't override what I know deep down.

If you don't trust yourself yet, you can build that. One honest decision at a time.

8. Allow yourself to be seen.

This is deeper than just asking for help. Because asking for help is one thing—but allowing yourself to be seen while doing it... that's the real work.

There were so many moments in my life when I needed support, but I stayed quiet. I handled it on my own. I told myself I was fine.

Not because I didn't need help—but because being seen felt vulnerable.

Healing changed that.

I started asking for help. From my therapist. From my safe humans. From my publisher and editor.

From the mentors and tools God placed in my life. From Andrea, a stranger turned angel, who walked with me through a season when I truly needed support.

Even in quiet ways, I reached for it. With Mama B. With safe people.

With God.

And every single time I did..., it expanded me.

It took me to the next level of healing. The next level of growth. The next level of becoming.

Asking for help didn't make me weak—it allowed me to become who I was becoming.

Some of the most beautiful relationships in my life came from me being willing to say, "I need support here."

So, if you've been carrying everything on your own... You don't have to.

9. You get to make things special.

This is something I didn't understand for a long time.

I thought meaning had to be given to me. That things were only special if everyone else agreed they were. That significance had to be big, obvious, or universally understood.

But healing showed me something different. You get to make things special. You get to take a date, a number, a moment—and give it meaning.

You get to attach something sacred to your life simply because it matters to you.

For me, April 16 means everything. It's the day I was baptized. The day I went under the water and released so much shame... so much weight... so much of what I had been carrying.

And when I came up—I was different.

Years later, I felt that same pull to that date again. I remember thinking, *Wouldn't it be so special to release my book on April 16?* It didn't unfold that way. Life was shifting. The timing didn't quite line up.

But I've learned something about meaning—it doesn't disappear just because the outcome changes. So I honored it anyway. I went to a quiet place in Arizona a space that Invited stillness, reflection, and God. I gave myself time to pause… to breathe... To come back to myself.

And in that space—I honored it—by choosing myself, my healing, and God.

Through all the changes, all the healing, all the unknowns—I spoke it out loud. I asked. And it was honored.

April 16 became the day my memoir would be released.

And to anyone else, it might just look like a date on a calendar. But to me—it holds transformation. Surrender. Obedience. Becoming.

That's what I want you to know: you don't have to wait for something to be labeled special.

You get to create that. You get to notice the ordinary moments—and make them meaningful. You get to honor the signs, the numbers, and the memories that feel significant to your heart.

Even if no one else understands it. There is something powerful about choosing to see your life that way.

So, if something feels special to you… hold onto it. Let it mean something.

You're allowed to do that.

This is your permission slip.

If a part of you is still waiting for permission to live a life that feels true to you… Let this be it.

You are allowed.

You are allowed to take people at face value.

You are allowed to choose healing.

You are allowed to listen to yourself.

You are allowed to make the right decision—even when it feels hard.

You are allowed to be still.

You are allowed to trust yourself.

You are allowed to be seen.

You are allowed to create meaning in your life.

This is my gift to you.

Not just words—but lived experience.

I didn't just learn these things.

I practiced them. I fought for them. I became because of them.

And everything you've read… everything I've lived… has led me here.

To a place where I'm not just becoming—I'm embodying who I am. And you can, too.

CHAPTER 42

What I See Now

This is what keeps happening as I write this book.

Moments I remembered but didn't understand are revealing their meaning. Lessons that lived quietly in my body are rising to the surface with clarity and truth. And I can finally see how much goodness my father gave me—how much wisdom I was carrying even when I didn't know it.

I don't have to cling to the painful memories to honor the story.

I get to choose what I keep.

There are moments in healing when something settles—not with force, but with certainty. This was one of those moments—a quiet internal shift.

A pause. A quiet internal shift. Nothing dramatic. Just clear.

I've come to recognize the difference between reacting from old patterns and responding from something deeper. Now, I can pause. I can listen. I can let the noise settle long enough to hear what's actually true.

Not every part of me needs to be followed.

And for the first time, I trust the part of me that does.

We're not doing that. Not because I can't—but because I won't.

The old version of me would have reached out, hoping for support, even if it meant abandoning myself in the process. I don't judge her. I understand her.

But the woman I am now chooses differently.

I don't want provision that comes with control, silence, or erasure. I want the kind that aligns with who I am becoming. I trust God with that—even when it stretches me.

So, I paused. I listened. I didn't shame the part of me that was trying to solve it.

And then my core answered.

This is what healing looks like. The parts don't disappear—they just stop running the show.

And the biggest difference?

I no longer live in shame.

If someone asked me what I no longer use to make decisions, my answer would be simple.

Shame.

And that changes everything.

CHAPTER 43

I'm Not Carrying Shame Anymore

If there's one thing I'm no longer willing to live with, it's shame.

It took me years to understand how deeply it shaped me—my thoughts, my actions, my decisions, my relationships, and the way I saw myself. And now that I see it, I can't unsee it.

Shame didn't always feel loud. Most of the time, it showed up quietly—through overexplaining, minimizing, shrinking, and second-guessing myself. It showed up when I wanted to use my voice, speak my truth, or stand up for myself, and somehow that felt wrong. That felt shameful.

It was woven into the smallest moments. Even something as simple as rest felt loaded. If my body needed to slow down, there was a voice attached to it—lazy, unproductive, not enough.

The words themselves weren't always extreme, but the tone carried something deeper. Disapproval. Dismissal. Shame.

Over time, my body learned that language.

When you grow up with even subtle emotional correction or manipulation, your body adapts quickly. It learns what feels safe and what doesn't. It learns how to avoid discomfort, how to stay small, and how to not feel too much. That conditioning doesn't just live in your thoughts—it lives in your nervous system.

For a long time, I didn't have language for any of this. I just knew how to function inside of it.

Healing changed that.

It forced me to slow down enough to actually notice what I had been living with. To be honest with myself about how I was functioning and what was driving my decisions. I started to recognize that the patterns I had normalized were actually painful to my system. They weren't protecting me anymore—they were limiting me.

Through therapy, journaling, and EMDR, something began to shift. I would leave sessions and write, and I could feel the difference—not just in what I was thinking, but in how I was experiencing myself. My thoughts began to change. My body began to respond differently.

And I realized something I had never fully seen before: So much of what I had been carrying… wasn't mine.

That was a turning point. Because once I could see it, I had a choice.

And I made a decision:

I'm not doing shame anymore.

That doesn't mean it never shows up. Healing doesn't erase everything overnight. Triggers still happen. Old thoughts still try to surface. There are still moments where I can feel the pull of old conditioning.

But it doesn't lead me anymore. That's the difference.

I can see it now. I can pause. I can choose differently.

And that choice is changing everything—not just for me, but for my daughter.

Shame is one of the biggest cycles I am committed to breaking. Because I can already see how easily it transfers. How quickly it can shape the way a child sees themselves, their worth, their voice, and their needs.

And I won't pass that on.

We talk about rest in our home. We talk about our feelings. We talk about our nervous system. We talk about what it means to be human without attaching shame to it.

There are moments when I can feel my old conditioning try to rise up—where my instinct is to correct, to control, to respond the way it was modeled for me.

And I stop.

Because I'm aware now. And that awareness gives me the ability to choose something different.

This is what breaking generational cycles looks like in real life. It's not perfect. It's not polished. It's intentional.

My daughter is not going to inherit the emotional patterns I had to spend years unraveling.

She's going to inherit awareness, safety, and the freedom to be fully herself. That is the inheritance I'm choosing to leave.

Shame may have been a part of my story, but it does not get to define my future—or hers.

CHAPTER 44

Social Media and Self-Abandonment

As a healed woman, I've noticed things I never imagined I would, especially around social media. I don't believe social media is bad. I think everything is relative. Technology itself isn't the problem. Presence is. Compulsion is. What we unconsciously put first is.

For years, I grabbed my phone the moment I woke up. Alarm. Notifications. Messages. Scrolling. Business. Other people's lives—before my own. And I didn't think twice about it because that's what everyone did. It was normal. Automatic. Conditioned.

What I had to unlearn... slowly, intentionally..., was this: everyone and everything else came first.

That realization alone changed everything.

I'm not here to shame anyone. I'm not saying checking your phone is wrong. What I am saying is that, when you wake up and immediately enter everyone else's world, your nervous system doesn't belong to you yet. You're stepping straight into comparison, stimulation, performance, and noise—before your own body has even had a chance to breathe.

And yes, I always hear Brendon Burchard in my head when I think about this—arms flailing, full of enthusiasm, saying something like, "When you scroll, your brain is comparing a million times a minute."

And he's not wrong. If you know Brendon, you know exactly what I mean. *DDDDD*. Full sound effects and all.

Whether we like it or not, scrolling is comparison. Even subtle comparison. Even "inspiration." Your brain is tracking, measuring, and absorbing. You are stepping into other people's moods, lives, highlights, and narratives—before anchoring into your own.

What surprised me most in my healing wasn't that I wanted more boundaries online. It was how little I needed to be seen.

That realization stunned me.

For a long time, social media had been a validation tool—whether I wanted to admit it or not. Admiration regulated my nervous system temporarily. Attention soothed something in me that didn't yet know how to self-soothe. I don't judge that version of myself. She was doing the best she could with what she knew. But healing changed the equation.

I wanted choice instead of compulsion.

Regulation instead of validation.

Presence instead of performance.

When everything broke open in my life—my family, my faith, my identity, and my understanding of safety—I didn't know how to show up online without pretending I had answers that I didn't have. So sometimes, I didn't show up at all. Other times, I showed up honestly but quietly. Still here.

Still human. Just no longer performing my way into worthiness.

And here's the truth that shocked me most: being offline used to scare me.

Now, it feels like relief.

While writing this book, I stepped away for days at a time. No scrolling. No posting. No checking. And nothing bad happened. My world didn't collapse. I didn't disappear. My body learned—over and over—that I was safe without being witnessed.

That's how nervous systems heal. Through repetition. Through proof. Through lived experience.

The more I reminded my body that I was okay, the more it believed me.

We absorb more than we realize. The people we're around. The content we consume. The voices we listen to. The stories we scroll. The emotions we take in without noticing. What you watch, you absorb. What you absorb, you become—at least a little.

Social media can absolutely be used for good. I've experienced real connection, education, spiritual growth, and community through it. I love technology. I'm grateful I can FaceTime my daughter. I'm grateful for the ways it has expanded access and understanding.

But it can also be a quiet detriment to our emotional and mental health—especially when we're already dysregulated, exhausted, or healing.

Here's what I know now: what you absorb matters.

Not just physically—but emotionally, mentally, and spiritually. The people you're around. The stories you scroll.

The content you take in. The tone of your environment. All of it leaves an imprint.

There's a reason they say you become the five people you spend the most time with. It's not motivational fluff—it's nervous system truth. Your body learns what's normal from proximity. From repetition. From exposure. From what it sees, hears, and feels every single day.

We don't just witness our environment—we internalize it.

Not just the weather. Not just the news. But the people, the energy, the pace, and the noise. You get to decide whether your life begins with presence or comparison. With your own breath—or everyone else's highlight reel.

Healing taught me that I don't need to be admired to be safe. And I would rather feel safe in my body than validated online any day.

I believe this deeply: when you know better, you do better. If the light turns on, you don't shove it back under the rug. You look. You adjust. You choose again.

And that choice—over and over—is where healing lives.

CHAPTER 45

Living from Safety

Some mornings, when I pause and take in my life, I still feel a quiet disbelief—not because it looks extraordinary from the outside, but because it feels so different than the way I was taught to live.

Right now, my daughter is still asleep. It's late morning, and I'm completely at peace with that. There was a time when that would've filled me with shame. I was conditioned to believe rest meant laziness, productivity equaled worth, and slowing down was something you earned only after you proved yourself. We didn't listen to our bodies. We overrode them. We pushed through.

But I know something different now, not because I read it somewhere, but because my own healing demanded it. Rest heals at a cellular level. Over the last two years, I have rested more than I had in the decade before—real rest, the kind that doesn't come from exhaustion but from safety. And with it came clarity, regulation, and a steadiness I had never known. Now, I give that same permission to my daughter, not as an experiment, not as rebellion, but as a conscious, grounded choice.

For a long time, I was great at routines. Disciplined. Committed. I knew how to show up, perform, push, and achieve. There was value in that season. Structure matters. Tools matter. But it wasn't healing. It was conditioning. And conditioning can look a lot like healing when you've spent your life surviving.

I learned the affirmations, built the habits, stayed consistent, looked strong on the outside—yet none of it reached my nervous system. It didn't teach my body it was safe. It didn't interrupt the survival patterns running quietly underneath everything.

I once heard my therapist say you can tell yourself you're worthy every day and it might help, but until your body believes it, nothing truly changes. That was the turning point. Real healing isn't stacking better routines on top of survival. It's dismantling survival and learning how to live without it.

That's what these last years have been for me. Not self-improvement. Integration. That's why retreats mattered, why nature mattered, why horses mattered, why Costa Rica mattered. Because those experiences didn't just teach me something new. They reintroduced my body to safety. I didn't just understand calm, I felt it, and once your body knows that difference, there's no going back. Now, I'm living from that place and parenting from it, too.

There was a time when I loved my daughter fiercely, but I was still living from survival. I showed up for her constantly, but I didn't yet understand how much a mother's nervous system shapes a child's inner world. I can see it clearly now without shame, without self-blame, because healing isn't punishing who you were; it's taking responsibility for who you're becoming.

Somewhere along the way, I realized something that keeps proving itself true: it's not *what* I know, it's *who* I know, and in this season, it's who I'm doing this with—God, my core self, and the people He's placed around me. The tools matter, yes, but what matters more is who you're anchored to while you use those tools.

My daughter watches me rest. She watches me pause. She watches me choose steadiness over urgency. Sometimes, she's confused, because it's new, so we walk it together.

I'll say, "We don't have to do it like that anymore."

And I can see her nervous system soften before her mind fully understands.

That's how healing works. It changes what feels normal. This isn't loud. It isn't performative. It isn't something I need to explain or defend. It's embodied. It's honest. And it's the most grounded version of myself I've ever lived.

And still there's a part of me that pauses when I share this, a quiet wondering if I'm allowed to speak with this kind of clarity, if I'm "far enough healed" to name what I now understand.

And that question tells me something important. It tells me I'm no longer speaking from performance or certainty but from awareness.

Because alongside that questioning part is another one—steady, intelligent, and deeply grounded—reminding me of the truth. I've lived both extremes. I've lived the life of conditioning and the life of integration. I've functioned from survival, and now I live from regulation.

Clarity doesn't always come with instructions. It comes with responsibility. And responsibility can feel heavy when you've spent a lifetime carrying things that were never yours to begin with. I didn't suddenly know what to do with all this awareness. I just knew I couldn't unknow it. I couldn't unsee the patterns. I couldn't unfeel the misalignment. I couldn't pretend the old pathways still fit.

This is the part of healing people don't talk about—the space where nothing is fully resolved, but everything is illuminated. The part where you are still grieving, still struggling, still uncertain—and yet unmistakably awake.

Awareness is the gift. And it is also the threshold.

Because once the light is on, you're standing at a doorway. Behind you is the familiar—the coping, the proving, the performing, and the self-sacrifice that once kept you safe. Ahead of you is something quieter and braver: *choice.* Choice grounded in truth. Choice rooted in the body. Choice guided by God instead of fear.

Healing didn't hand me a new life overnight. It handed me discernment. And discernment changed everything.

I didn't blow my life up overnight. I didn't make dramatic declarations. I didn't even fully trust myself yet. What I did was quieter. I started noticing. And once I noticed, my body refused to go back to sleep.

That was the beginning of the end—not of my marriage, but of my ability to survive by silence.

There was a season when nothing mattered more than my daughter's emotional safety. Every decision I made ran through one filter: *Will this protect her nervous system*? We went to therapy every week. We moved slowly. We spoke gently. I swallowed ego and chose steadiness over reaction. I walked through the hardest transition of my life with one anchor—integrity.

That season was about gentle intention. It wasn't loud. It wasn't performative. It was sacred, and I am proud of the woman who carried it. But then, something shifted.

One day, I looked around and realized we were living in the haven I had prayed for. The house felt safe. My body felt quieter. My daughter felt steadier. And I was fully responsible for both of us. We had crossed something. And for the first time in my life, survival wasn't the goal anymore. Building was.

This year is not about escaping pain. It's about embodying peace. It's about celebrating sixteen years sober without shrinking it, about publishing a book and actually letting myself feel proud, and about traveling not to run but to expand, creating new traditions because I am allowed to.

Last season was surrender. This season is surrender and celebration. Last season was gentle intention. This season is gentle action. I am not running toward another relationship. I am not scrambling for validation. I am building a fortress—grounded, soft, and sovereign.

And for the first time in my life, I trust myself to drive the bus. It's a beautiful bus. And I'm not going back.

I didn't come to this understanding from a distance. I lived it. I felt it in my body, over time, in ways I couldn't rush or bypass.

So this isn't about having all the answers or claiming I've arrived somewhere final. It's about telling the truth from where I stand now—with honesty, with humility, and with a deep respect for the process it took to get here.

And if anything that I've shared offers even a small sense of language, relief, or permission to someone else… then it has already done exactly what it was meant to do.

I didn't need instructions.
I needed the courage to follow what
God had already made clear.

CHAPTER 46

Hope, Grace, and Surrender

Releasing this book will cost me something. I can already feel that.

I don't yet know the full price—whether it's financial, relational, reputational, or emotional—but I know this much: alignment always asks for something in return.

When you offer something sacred to the world… when you tell the truth with your whole chest, when you stop editing yourself for safety or approval, there is a cost.

And I'm willing to pay it.

Because what lives on the other side of that cost—the meaning, the obedience, the beauty, the blessing—is worth more than whatever I'm releasing.

Writing this book, becoming an author, and offering these pages to God, to other humans, and to myself, is something I never thought I could do.

And yet, here I am, doing it anyway.

Not because it's easy…

but because God placed it on my heart, and I trust where He's leading me.

But because it's right.

Over the last few years of healing and integration—of slowly rewiring my nervous system and learning how to live inside my body again—three words kept returning to me. Not as slogans or quotes, but as lived necessities. They became the framework that carried me through the darkest parts of this journey.

Hope.

Grace.

Surrender.

Hope came first, because it had to. When your life collapses in ways you didn't choose, when betrayal and trauma destabilize everything that you thought was solid, then hope is not optimism—it's survival. Hope is the small light you grab when you cannot see the way out. It's choosing to believe something exists beyond the pain, even when you have no evidence yet. For survivors, hope is not optional. It's life.

Grace followed, because hope alone isn't enough. You have to give yourself permission to be a mess. To grieve in waves. To fall apart. To move slowly. To not have answers. Grace is what allows you to heal without shaming yourself for how long it takes. It's remembering that, when your world is upside down, you're not supposed to be composed—you're supposed to be human.

And then came surrender—the hardest and most transformative of all.

Surrender wasn't giving up. It was letting go of my obsession with control. It was releasing the need to understand every outcome, manage every emotion, and predict every next step. It was learning to listen instead of force. To respond instead of react. To follow the quiet whispers instead of the loud fear.

Hope kept me alive.

Grace kept me soft.

Surrender changed everything.

Together, they became my equation for healing.

If there is anything I want to leave you with, it's this: everything you need is already inside of you. Not as a hollow affirmation or something to repeat until it feels true—but as a reality that becomes accessible when you learn how to listen. When you stop outsourcing your worth. When you reconnect to your body, your spirit, and the faith that anchors you.

Healing doesn't come from becoming someone new.

It comes from returning to who you already are.

So, I offer this to you—not as instruction, but as invitation. You can come back to these pages whenever you forget. Whenever the road feels unclear. Whenever the cost feels heavy.

You are enough.

You are chosen.

You are exactly where you're meant to be—even when it feels terrifying, even when it feels like everything is falling apart.

Hope will carry you.
Grace will hold you.
And surrender will lead you.

CHAPTER 47

The Doorway

What I'm learning is that becoming doesn't happen all at once. It happens in motion—while walking, while grieving, while advocating, while trusting God in places that still feel unfinished. And sometimes, without fanfare, you realize you've stepped into something new.

There are moments in life that don't announce themselves as endings or beginnings—they just feel different in your body. Quieter. Wider. Like something has shifted even though nothing on the outside looks dramatic yet.

This is one of those moments.

I am not who I was when this story began. I'm not even who I was a year ago. I've walked through betrayal, grief, identity collapse, and the slow, painstaking work of healing childhood wounds I didn't even know had names. I've learned how trauma lives in the nervous system. I've learned how to feel instead of flee. I've learned how to listen to my body and trust my intuition—and how to surrender when I don't have answers.

Three years ago, I went no-contact with my mother and watched the foundation of my entire life crack open. Not just a fracture—but a full unraveling.

Everything I thought I knew about who I was, where I came from, and what love meant had to be reexamined. There was no way back to innocence—only forward into truth.

And that truth was the hardest thing I had ever faced.

That journey was grueling. Dissecting. At times, it felt like everything was falling apart. And yet—somehow—it was only a beginning.

It pulled me deeper into my faith.

It brought wounds To the surface I had never named. It asked more of me than I ever thought I could give.

And slowly—it began to change me.

And now, here I am.

My marriage has come to an end. My home is changing. My daughter and I are building something new together—something softer, safer, and more honest. I am homeschooling her not because I have it all figured out, but because I know what her nervous system needs. I know what safety feels like now. I know what love looks like when it is steady instead of conditional.

Some doors closed quietly.

Some slammed.

Some, I had to pry open myself.

And then, something became clear: I didn't arrive here by accident.

Three years of unraveling what was never true.

Three years of learning how trauma lived in my body.

Three years of sitting in therapy rooms and trusting that God could meet me even in the places I didn't want to look.

And now, I stand in the quiet aftermath—not finished, not fully healed, but awake.

The old version of me survived. This one is choosing to live.

I am building a new rhythm of safety. I am listening for God's whispers instead of the world's noise. I am surrendering control—not because I am weak, but because I am finally strong enough to trust what I cannot yet see.

There are still things that hurt. There are still things that feel unjust. There is still money, grief, and the residue of a life I had to leave behind.

But there is also something else now.

Peace.

Faith.

A future that no longer terrifies me.

This story doesn't end with everything tied in a bow. It ends with me standing in a doorway—not frozen, not afraid—but breathing. Surrendered. Ready.

And somewhere beyond this page, another story is already beginning.

There is a cost to not being believed. It doesn't just wound your feelings—it alters your nervous system. It teaches your body to doubt its own signals. It teaches your mind to second-guess reality. It makes you work overtime trying to prove something that should never have required proof.

For me, that cost showed up as anxiety, confusion, and eventually CPTSD. My system learned to scan, to brace, to anticipate. It learned that safety depended on performance and explanation.

But healing didn't come from proving my story. It came from being believed.

By God.

By safe people.

And, eventually, by myself.

I no longer needed to convince. I no longer needed to argue for my own experience.

The relief of not having to defend my truth wasn't loud—it was steady. It was the beginning of peace.

I wasn't entirely sure where to end this book. In truth, I still have so much to say. Healing from divorce has opened layers of wisdom I never could have understood without walking through the pain myself.

Motherhood continues to unfold right in front of me with new challenges, heavy decisions, and moments that stretch my heart in ways both beautiful and terrifying. Life keeps moving. There will always be more stories, more lessons, more healing to share.

For a while, it was hard for me to stop writing. Every time I thought I was nearing the end, another piece of life would open up and ask to be told. But my mentor reminded me of something simple and wise: a book doesn't have to hold the whole story. It only needs to hold the truth of where you are right now. The rest will come later. Other chapters. Other books.

So, I accepted that this manuscript is a marker in time—an honest reflection of what I've walked through, what I've learned, and what I'm ready to share today.

Still, I wondered how the story should close.

And then, something happened that I could never have planned.

For weeks, I had been trying to locate the phone number of Dixie Madden, the attorney who represented me when I was a little girl. The woman in the blue suit who rode up the elevator with me before we walked into that courtroom. The one who somehow brought a small sense of calm to a frightened child on a day I barely remember, except for her.

I had carried the memory of Dixie for more than thirty years. I wasn't even sure she was real for a long time. Memory can play strange tricks when trauma is involved. But one thing remained clear: a woman who looked at me with kindness when I needed it most.

So, I asked around. Weeks passed, and nothing happened. Then, one morning, her name and number appeared in my inbox.

The date was March 16.

Of all the days.

The same date that already carried meaning in my life—my baptism anniversary, the day that reminds me how God rewrote the direction of my story.

I sat there, staring at the email, smiling in disbelief. After thirty-five years, her name had found its way back to me—on that day.

I didn't need anything from her. I simply felt a pull to reach out and say thank you. To let her know that the little girl she once stood up for had never forgotten her.

So, I sent the message. And then I waited.

When she wrote back, she apologized and explained she was retired now and no longer practicing law. She thought I was asking for help.

I wrote again and told her the truth—that I wasn't looking for counsel. I only wanted to thank her. That I remembered her. That I had carried that memory into adulthood. That it mattered more than she could know.

Not long after, another message came. She told me my words meant so much to her. That hearing from me gave her a sense of purpose and meaning for the way she had always hoped to live and work.

I sat there, reading her message, as tears streamed down my face, feeling something settle deep inside my heart. After all these years, a small circle had closed.

The little girl who once walked into that courtroom had finally been able to say thank you. And the woman who once stood beside her now knew that her presence had mattered.

I could not have written a better ending to this story if I'd tried. Because that moment reminded me of something I've come to believe with my whole heart:

God goes before us.

Even when we cannot see it.

Even when years pass between the chapters.

He arranges moments we could never orchestrate ourselves. He ties together threads from the past and places them in front of us at exactly the right time.

I hadn't spoke to her —not once since I was a little girl. More than thirty years had passed.

Sometimes, the most meaningful endings aren't dramatic at all. Sometimes, they look like an email arriving on an ordinary morning. Sometimes, they look like a message sent across thirty-five years.

And sometimes, they look like the quiet realization that the people who helped carry you through your hardest moments were never forgotten.

Know what will come next. I know how quickly everything can change—how life can shift in an instant.

But I also know this: healing changes you. And with God, it can change the trajectory of your life in ways you never could have imagined. I stand by that wholeheartedly. I would not be the woman writing these words sharing this story this honestly this vulnerably—if that weren't true.

So, if you are walking through something difficult right now—something that feels unfinished or unresolved—I want you to know this: beautiful things can grow on the other side of hard chapters.

You may not see how the story comes together yet. You may not know where your ending will land. But that doesn't mean it isn't being written.

If you're struggling to believe that today, you're welcome to borrow my belief for a little while.

I had to borrow someone else's once, too.

The story is still unfolding—and so are you, in ways you may not even see yet.

CLOSING WHISPER

This version is enough.
Not because the story is finished…
but because I finally told the truth.
The rest will come.

ACKNOWLEDGMENTS

This story may have my name on it—but it was never mine to hold alone. I was carried—by people, by love, and by God in ways both seen and unseen.

At the heart of it all is my daughter Maddie—you are the reason I chose to heal, to grow, and to become the version of myself I want you to experience. I love you more than words can hold.

To the people God placed in my life at exactly the right time—my therapists, mentors, and guides: thank you for helping me come home to myself.

To my publisher, editor, and Raina: thank you for your guidance, your care, and your belief in this story—for going first, showing me what was possible, and helping me shape these words with integrity and intention.

To Andrea, for walking with me in such a sacred season and reminding me what safety feels like in real time.

To the friends and chosen family who supported me in quiet and powerful ways—you know who you are.

And to Molly, my sweet boxer, my constant companion through the writing, the healing, and the in-between moments, thank you for being my steady grounding presence.

And most importantly, to God, for never leaving me, for guiding every step, and for turning my story into something meaningful.

ABOUT THE AUTHOR

Tammy Blake is a writer, mother, and cycle-breaker whose work centers on healing, nervous-system regulation, and faith-led transformation. Her journey began in performance and survival—driven, capable, and resilient—until she recognized how deeply those patterns were rooted in childhood trauma rather than safety.

Through years of deep healing work, including EMDR and parts integration, Tammy began to reconnect to her voice, her body, and her truth. Her work now explores what it means to move from survival to safety, and to break generational cycles by choosing awareness, faith, and emotional freedom.

This memoir was born from lived experience, faith, and embodiment, offering an honest exploration of CPTSD, identity, and what it means to build a life rooted in truth instead of survival. She lives with her daughter and continues writing, healing, and creating spaces where clarity, peace, and courage can grow.

www.ingramcontent.com/pod-product-compliance
Lightning Source LLC
LaVergne TN
LVHW091032080826
845145LV00002B/464

* 9 7 8 1 9 5 9 9 5 5 8 5 6 *